Digital SAT

Practice Questions 2025

The Complete Guide Featuring 790 Exercises with In-Depth Explanations for Every Answer and Insights to Boost Test-Day Readiness

Ultra Prep Publications

Disclaimer

This book is designed to provide information about the digital SAT exam as of the date of publication. It is sold with the understanding that the publisher and author are not engaged in rendering legal, accounting, or other professional services. While the publisher and author have used their best efforts in preparing this book, they make no representations or warranties with respect to the accuracy or completeness of the contents of this book and specifically disclaim any implied warranties of merchantability or fitness for a particular purpose. No warranty may be created or extended by sales representatives or written sales materials.

SAT® is a registered trademark of the College Board, which was not involved in the production of, and does not endorse, this product. This book is not sponsored or endorsed by, or affiliated with, the College Board or ETS. All trademarks, service marks, registered trademarks, and registered service marks are the property of their respective owners and are used herein for identification purposes only.

TABLE OF CONTENTS

INTRODUCTON

Overview of the Digital SAT: Changes and Trends

The SAT has undergone a significant transformation with its shift to a fully digital, adaptive format, officially rolling out for U.S. students in 2024. This modernization addresses accessibility and ease-of-use concerns while aiming to reduce testing stress, making it a streamlined alternative to the traditional paper format.

The new digital SAT is shorter, now approximately two hours long compared to the previous three-hour duration. The exam is divided into two main sections—**Reading and Writing, and Math**—with each section split into adaptive modules. Adaptive testing means that the questions adjust in difficulty based on a student's performance, allowing the test to be completed in less time without compromising its evaluative rigor. This new approach also allows for faster scoring, with results expected within days rather than weeks, greatly benefiting students and admissions timelines.

In the Reading and Writing section, the format now features short passages (25-150 words each) with single questions per passage, replacing the longer, multi-question texts from the previous SAT. This format simplifies comprehension and focuses on concise understanding and application, which has been welcomed as a positive change by early test-takers. Additionally, College Board has introduced some new question types, such as those that require synthesizing information from brief notes, and has removed certain elements like idiomatic expressions and commonly confused words to reduce test anxiety.

The Math section has also seen notable adjustments. Students can now use calculators throughout both modules, either using their own or accessing the Desmos calculator provided on the digital platform. The question format maintains a mix of multiple-choice and student-response types, but there's no longer a distinction between calculator-permitted and non-calculator segments. Topics such as imaginary and complex numbers have been eliminated, ensuring a more focused approach to core concepts.

With each test being uniquely generated from a large question pool, the digital format greatly enhances security, reducing risks of test leaks or collaboration attempts. Furthermore, the SAT's digital nature provides students with helpful tools like an on-screen timer, highlighters, and answer-elimination options, supporting them as they navigate through the exam more effectively.

This shift not only reflects a response to changing educational needs but also acknowledges the increased adoption of test-optional policies. The adaptive and digital nature of the new SAT offers a fairer, more accessible testing experience designed to suit a wider range of student needs and learning styles.

Purpose and Structure of the Digital SAT

The Digital SAT represents a shift in standardized testing to better match the modern needs of students and institutions. This digital format not only reduces the test duration to approximately two hours and fourteen minutes but also introduces a modular, adaptive structure, making the test shorter and potentially more focused for each student. The test is divided into two primary sections: Reading and Writing and Math. Each section includes two adaptive modules, and within each module, question difficulty adjusts based on a student's performance in real-time. This adaptive approach aims to enhance fairness and efficiency by challenging students at a level that reflects their ability.

In sum, the Digital SAT's purpose is to provide a streamlined, secure, and adaptive testing environment that accurately reflects each student's skill level while keeping pace with modern educational trends.

Scoring and Benchmarking of the Digital SAT

The scoring structure of the Digital SAT maintains a familiar total score range of 400 to 1600, calculated as the sum of two section scores: Reading and Writing and Math, each on a 200-800 scale. This structure allows students and colleges to assess performance consistently across different testing formats. However, with its new adaptive format, each section is split into two modules, where performance on the first module determines the difficulty of the second, aiming to more precisely measure each student's abilities.

In each section, students encounter a balanced mix of easy, medium, and difficult questions in the first module. Based on their responses, the second module adjusts to present either a more challenging or easier set of questions. This adaptivity means that more difficult questions generally contribute more toward the final score, so students are incentivized to answer as many initial questions correctly as possible to reach the highest scoring potential. However, College Board ensures scoring fairness across test versions through a process called "score equating," which adjusts for variations in test difficulty between test dates and modules.

College Board has set college readiness benchmarks for the Digital SAT to help identify students who are prepared for college-level work. A score of 480 in Reading and Writing and 530 in Math indicates college readiness, signaling that students who meet or exceed these benchmarks are more likely to succeed in entry-level college courses. This benchmark remains consistent with the previous paper-based test to provide continuity in college readiness metrics.

In addition to total and section scores, students receive detailed feedback across core domains within each section. In Reading and Writing, this includes areas such as Information and Ideas, Craft and Structure, and Standard English Conventions. In Math, students are evaluated on skills across Algebra, Advanced Math, Problem Solving, and Geometry. This breakdown helps students understand strengths and areas for improvement if retaking the test. Many colleges also use these scores to benchmark applicants and evaluate eligibility for scholarships, often favoring scores that align with their admitted student averages. For instance, top-tier colleges generally look for scores of 1400 or higher, while a score above 1200 is typically competitive for many institutions.

The digital SAT's adaptive format and detailed scoring feedback aim to provide a nuanced picture of student readiness, benefiting both students and admissions offices in making informed, data-backed decisions.

How to Use This Book Effectively

The practice questions in this book have been crafted to reflect the types of questions likely to appear on the new digital SAT. They closely mirror the anticipated structure, focus areas, and difficulty level across Reading, Writing, and Math, giving you a realistic preview of what to expect on test day. By working steadily through these exercises, you'll strengthen the skills necessary for success on the exam.

Begin with the sections where you feel additional practice will be most beneficial. When reviewing your responses, pay particular attention to explanations for any questions you missed. Understanding these will allow you to zero in on the specific skills each module of the test emphasizes. With focus and dedication, you'll be well-prepared to tackle the SAT. Best of luck!

CHAPTER 1

Digital SAT Format and Adaptive Testing

Introduction to Digital SAT Modules

The Digital SAT is structured around a modular, adaptive format that is distinct from the traditional paper-based test. It is divided into two main sections—Reading and Writing and Math—and each section is broken into two modules. Each module is designed to progressively adapt to the student's performance, ensuring the exam challenges each test-taker at an appropriate level.

Structure and Timing of Modules

In the Reading and Writing section, each module consists of 27 questions to be completed within 32 minutes, covering skills in vocabulary, reading comprehension, and grammar. These questions focus on short, manageable passages, unlike the longer texts of the previous SAT, allowing students to demonstrate quick comprehension and application of knowledge. The Math section includes two modules as well, each with 22 questions and a 35-minute limit. Math questions range from algebra and problem-solving to geometry, and a calculator is permitted throughout this section.

Questions in the Reading and Writing section fall into categories such as:

- Words in Context
- Structure and Purpose
- Main Ideas and Details
- Quantitative Evidence
- Textual Evidence
- Inferences

Writing questions cover areas including Verb Agreement, Punctuation, Sentence Structure and Organization, Transitions, and Rhetorical Analysis of Notes.

Questions in the Math section include both multiple-choice and student-response formats and cover topics like:

- Algebra
- Problem Solving and Data Analysis
- Advanced Math.

This structure allows the SAT to assess a broader skill set efficiently, providing a targeted yet thorough evaluation of college readiness.

Once a module is completed, students cannot go back to it, as the performance on the first module determines the difficulty level of the second. Higher performance in the first module leads to more challenging questions in the second module, providing an opportunity for students to achieve higher scores. This adaptive system not only reduces the total testing time to around 2 hours and 14 minutes but also allows the SAT to provide a more tailored assessment experience.

Navigating the Modules and Tools

To support students, the digital SAT includes tools such as a digital timer, an on-screen calculator for the Math section, and annotation and elimination options to help highlight text and eliminate answers. These digital tools are embedded into the test interface, offering convenient, in-test strategies to manage time and focus on key details.

Overall, the modular setup and adaptive scoring system of the Digital SAT are designed to create a fairer, more dynamic testing experience that reflects students' abilities with a streamlined, efficient approach. For more details, explore resources from College Board, Princeton Review, and Test Innovators.

Computer-Based Testing Tools and Tips

The Digital SAT offers a suite of innovative tools within the Bluebook app, designed to make computer-based testing more accessible and user-friendly. Familiarizing yourself with these tools and tips for optimal usage can significantly enhance your test performance.

Key Testing Tools

- **Desmos Graphing Calculator:** Integrated into the Math section, this built-in graphing calculator allows you to perform calculations throughout both Math modules. This means there's no need to switch between different calculators, and you can graph equations, plot points, and perform various calculations right on-screen. However, if you prefer using a handheld calculator, you may bring one from the College Board's approved calculator list.

- **Countdown Clock:** A visible timer helps keep track of your progress in each section. You can choose to show or hide it based on your preference, but monitoring it can be a valuable way to ensure you're managing your time effectively across questions.

- **Math Reference Popout**: During the Math section, you'll have access to a reference sheet with essential formulas, covering topics like geometry and trigonometry. This popout eliminates the need to memorize every formula, allowing you to focus on solving problems rather than recalling equations.

- **Annotation and Mark-for-Review Options**: In the Reading and Writing section, you can highlight text, jot down notes, and mark questions for review if you want to revisit them before submitting the module. These features help you prioritize questions and quickly return to any flagged items within the module.

- **Online Notepad**: For students who prefer taking quick notes, an online notepad is available. This can be particularly useful for scratch work in Math or for summarizing key details in Reading and Writing passages.

Effective Tips for Using These Tools

- **Practice with the Bluebook App**: Downloading and practicing in the Bluebook app is essential. Full-length practice tests in this app mirror the adaptive format and question difficulty you'll encounter on test day, ensuring familiarity with each tool and feature. Practice navigating screens, using the calculator, and making the best use of mark-for-review options to develop a confident rhythm.

- **Use the Timer Wisely**: Consider using the countdown clock to pace yourself but avoid checking it too frequently, which can be distracting. Aim to keep a steady pace and be aware of time remaining as you approach the last few questions of each module.

- **Optimize the Calculator and Notepad**: Spend time getting comfortable with the Desmos calculator if you plan to use it, as knowing its functions will save time on test day. Additionally, use the notepad efficiently, particularly for complex math problems, so that all work remains organized and easily reviewable.

- **Take Advantage of Mark-for-Review**: Flag questions you find challenging, but avoid spending too much time on a single question. Mark it, move on, and return later if you have time. This approach will help ensure you maximize the number of questions you answer across both modules.

By familiarizing yourself with these tools, you'll be better prepared to handle the Digital SAT's unique format and leverage the test interface to your advantage. Practicing consistently with these tools in real-time will also enhance your comfort and efficiency on test day.

READING AND WRITING SECTION

CHAPTER 2

Reading Practice Questions

Words in Context

Understanding the meanings of words based on their context is a fundamental skill for tackling SAT Reading and Writing questions. In "Words in Context" exercises, the goal is to interpret unfamiliar vocabulary by examining the surrounding text for clues. This skill is crucial, as many SAT questions rely on your ability to understand nuanced language and choose the best word or phrase that aligns with the author's intent.

Context clues come in various forms, such as:

- **Definitions** embedded within the sentence itself
- **Examples** that help clarify a term's meaning
- **Comparisons** and **Contrasts** that shed light on a word's connotation
- **Restatements** and **Synonyms** that provide immediate substitutes
- **Details** that expand on the context to make meaning clearer

By analyzing these clues, you can gain a more precise understanding of challenging vocabulary, strengthening your reading comprehension. Practicing with these strategies will not only help you tackle SAT questions more effectively but will also enhance your vocabulary skills for academic reading. Now, let's explore some practice questions to build this skill further.

Questions

1. The artist's penchant for vibrant colors was evident in all his work, making each piece visually striking.

What does "penchant" most nearly mean?

(A) dislike

(B) tendency

(C) hesitation

(D) misunderstanding

2. Unlike his usual reticent nature, Mark was unusually loquacious at the party, chatting with nearly everyone.

What does "loquacious" most nearly mean?

(A) talkative

(B) reserved

(C) thoughtful

(D) shy

Why This Book Uses Concise Questions Without Full Passages

This book has been designed with concise questions that focus directly on core skills without providing full text passages. This approach allows readers to focus on essential SAT reading skills, such as identifying main ideas, analyzing structure, and understanding purpose, without becoming overwhelmed by extra details. For each question, the specific phrasing targets a distinct reading skill—whether it's discerning central ideas or making cross-text connections.

By practicing with focused questions, readers can develop the ability to efficiently extract meaning from complex texts, a critical skill for timed standardized tests like the SAT. This format is intended to simulate common question types without excessive reading load, helping readers stay on task and strengthen comprehension skills effectively.

3. The old library had a certain austere beauty, with minimal decoration and simple furnishings.

What does "austere" most nearly mean?

(A) joyful

(B) lively

(C) plain

(D) spacious

4. Although she appeared nonchalant, Sarah was actually quite nervous about the presentation.

What does "nonchalant" most nearly mean?

(A) anxious

(B) relaxed

(C) excited

(D) disorganized

5. The team's meticulous attention to detail led to a flawless project.

What does "meticulous" most nearly mean?

(A) careless

(B) thorough

(C) uncertain

(D) hesitant

6. Her succinct explanation of the complex theory impressed everyone.

What does "succinct" most nearly mean?

(A) lengthy

(B) unclear

(C) brief

(D) confusing

7. The young athlete's zeal for the sport was unmatched, driving her to practice every day.

What does "zeal" most nearly mean?

(A) dislike

(B) passion

(C) hesitation

(D) doubt

8. The unprecedented events led the community to take extra precautions.

What does "unprecedented" most nearly mean?

(A) unusual

(B) ignored

(C) common

(D) forgotten

9. Living near the placid lake provided a sense of peace and calm.

What does "placid" most nearly mean?

(A) noisy

(B) empty

(C) turbulent

(D) calm

10. Her decision was spontaneous, without much thought or planning.

What does "spontaneous" most nearly mean?

(A) calculated

(B) random

(C) organized

(D) scheduled

11. The scientist was known for her scrupulous research methods, which left no detail unexamined.

What does "scrupulous" most nearly mean?

(A) thorough

(B) careless

(C) doubtful

(D) slow

12. The author's speech was filled with platitudes that did little to inspire the audience.

What does "platitudes" most nearly mean?

(A) genuine emotions

(B) routine remarks

(C) arguments

(D) innovations

13. Despite the storm, the old cabin remained unscathed and intact.

What does "unscathed" most nearly mean?

(A) damaged

(B) visible

(C) unharmed

(D) abandoned

14. The poet's imagery was evocative, bringing powerful emotions to the surface.

What does "evocative" most nearly mean?

(A) forgettable

(B) stimulating

(C) detailed

(D) neutral

15. The ephemeral nature of the festival made it all the more precious to the villagers.

What does "ephemeral" most nearly mean?

(A) short-lived

(B) joyful

(C) frequent

(D) overwhelming

16. His attitude was intransigent, refusing to consider any suggestions from the team.

What does "intransigent" most nearly mean?

(A) flexible

(B) imaginative

(C) stubborn

(D) doubtful

17. The plant has adapted to the harsh desert climate, thriving despite minimal water.

What does "adapted" most nearly mean?

(A) moved

(B) survived

(C) adjusted

(D) wilted

18. The lawyer's argument was cogent, persuading even the most skeptical members of the jury.

What does "cogent" most nearly mean?

(A) weak

(B) irrelevant

(C) convincing

(D) tedious

19. The company's fortuitous success was unexpected but welcomed by all.

What does "fortuitous" most nearly mean?

(A) intentional

(B) accidental

(C) strategic

(D) inconsequential

20. The student was filled with trepidation before her final exam, fearing she hadn't studied enough.

What does "trepidation" most nearly mean?

(A) eagerness

(B) confusion

(C) fear

(D) confidence

21. The coach was venerated by all his players, respected for his knowledge and leadership.

What does "venerated" most nearly mean?

(A) ignored

(B) revered

(C) disrespected

(D) disliked

22. Her convoluted explanation only served to confuse the audience further."

What does "convoluted" most nearly mean?

(A) straightforward

(B) complex

(C) dull

(D) brief

23. The writer's story was filled with pathos, moving readers to tears.

What does "pathos" most nearly mean?

(A) excitement

(B) pity

(C) humor

(D) confusion

24. In her speech, the politician made veiled threats to those opposing her.

What does "veiled" most nearly mean?

(A) hidden

(B) direct

(C) gentle

(D) vague

25. The scientist's tenacious approach to research led her to a breakthrough discovery.

What does "tenacious" most nearly mean?

(A) hesitant

(B) persistent

(C) uncertain

(D) careless

26. The ambiguous instructions led to confusion among the students.

What does "ambiguous" most nearly mean?

(A) clear

(B) confusing

(C) fascinating

(D) detailed

27. The story's main character was a paragon of kindness and compassion.

What does "paragon" most nearly mean?

(A) example

(B) opposite

(C) critic

(D) beginner

28. Her perfunctory response made it clear she wasn't really interested in the project.

What does "perfunctory" most nearly mean?

(A) heartfelt

(B) interested

(C) superficial

(D) thorough

29. The ubiquitous presence of technology in modern life is undeniable.

What does "ubiquitous" most nearly mean?

(A) rare

(B) widespread

(C) excessive

(D) temporary

30. His stoic demeanor gave no hint of the stress he was under.

What does "stoic" most nearly mean?

(A) expressive

(B) detached

(C) passionate

(D) tense

Answer Explanations

1. (B) tendency – "Penchant" implies a strong liking or tendency, and the context suggests the artist consistently chooses vibrant colors.

2. (A) talkative – "Loquacious" describes someone who talks a lot, which contrasts with Mark's usual reticence.

3. (C) plain – "Austere" generally means simple or without luxury, fitting the description of the minimally decorated library.

4. (B) relaxed – "Nonchalant" means appearing calm and unconcerned, although Sarah is actually nervous.

5. (B) thorough – "Meticulous" implies extreme attention to detail, as indicated by the team's flawless project.

6. (C) brief – "Succinct" refers to concise and to-the-point communication, fitting Sarah's effective explanation.

7. (B) passion – "Zeal" denotes great enthusiasm, suitable for the athlete's commitment to practice.

8. (A) unusual – "Unprecedented" refers to something never seen before, explaining the need for extra precautions.

9. (D) calm – "Placid" suggests a serene, peaceful environment, matching the lake's impact on its surroundings.

10. (B) random – "Spontaneous" implies acting without premeditation, aligning with the unplanned nature of her decision.

11. (A) thorough – "Scrupulous" implies careful, precise attention to detail, indicating thoroughness.

12. (B) routine remarks – "Platitudes" are overused or unoriginal comments, typically lacking in inspiration.

13. (C) unharmed – "Unscathed" means not damaged, as suggested by "intact."

14. (B) stimulating – "Evocative" refers to something that brings strong feelings or images to mind.

15. (A) short-lived – "Ephemeral" means something that lasts for a very short time.

16. (C) stubborn – "Intransigent" suggests an unwillingness to compromise, showing stubbornness.

17. (C) adjusted – "Adapted" refers to adjusting or modifying to fit new conditions.

18. (C) convincing – "Cogent" indicates an argument that is clear and persuasive.

19. (B) accidental – "Fortuitous" implies happening by chance, often with a positive outcome.

20. (C) fear – "Trepidation" is a feeling of fear or anxiety about something.

21. (B) revered – "Venerated" means to regard with great respect.

22. (B) complex – "Convoluted" suggests something very intricate or complicated.

23. (B) pity – "Pathos" evokes emotions, especially sorrow or pity.

24. (A) hidden – "Veiled" suggests something that is disguised or not openly shown.

25. (B) persistent – "Tenacious" describes someone who does not give up easily.

26. (B) confusing – "Ambiguous" means something that can be understood in multiple ways, leading to confusion.

27. (A) example – "Paragon" refers to a perfect example or model of something.

28. (C) superficial – "Perfunctory" means doing something in a routine, unenthusiastic manner.

29. (B) widespread – "Ubiquitous" means found everywhere, commonly seen.

30. (B) detached – "Stoic" suggests remaining unaffected outwardly, regardless of emotions.

Structure and Purpose

Understanding a passage's structure and purpose is key to grasping its overall meaning. In the SAT Reading and Writing section, "Structure and Purpose" questions focus on analyzing why an author organized their ideas in a specific way and what message they aim to convey. This skill helps in discerning the effectiveness of different organizational techniques, such as cause-and-effect, problem-solution, or chronological order, as well as identifying the author's intentions, such as to inform, persuade, entertain, or reflect.

When analyzing structure, look for patterns like sequence, comparisons, contrasts, and evidence building. For purpose, consider why the author wrote the passage and how their tone and choice of words shape their message. These skills are valuable not only for SAT success but also for critical reading in academic and real-world contexts. Now, let's dive into some practice questions to apply these techniques.

Questions

1. The author outlines the process of erosion in coastal regions and discusses the roles of wind, water, and plants in shaping the landscape.

What is the primary purpose of this sentence?

(A) To argue against the impact of erosion on coastlines

(B) To describe the process and elements involved in coastal erosion

(C) To suggest that erosion is beneficial

(D) To highlight only the negative effects of erosion

2. The scientist's speech was straightforward and used practical examples, enabling her audience to grasp complex topics easily.

What is the primary function of this sentence?

(A) To describe how scientists communicate

(B) To explain why the audience had difficulty understanding

(C) To illustrate the speaker's effective communication style

(D) To criticize scientific jargon

3. The writer presents a series of questions to draw attention to the difficulties surrounding urban expansion.

What does this sentence indicate about the writer's approach?

(A) The writer focuses solely on solutions to urban issues

(B) The writer highlights complex problems with urban growth

(C) The writer offers a clear stance on the topic

(D) The writer avoids addressing any specific problems

4. In the passage, the author compares early explorers to modern-day travelers, showing both the similarities and vast differences in their experiences.

The main purpose of this comparison is to:

(A) Emphasize the advancements in travel technology

(B) Suggest that explorers and travelers share similar motives

(C) Contrast the challenges faced by each group

(D) Highlight the decline in exploration

5. The passage begins with an anecdote, setting a lighthearted tone before delving into serious issues.

What is the purpose of beginning with an anecdote?

(A) To create an amusing conclusion

(B) To undermine the topic's seriousness

(C) To engage readers before discussing complex topics

(D) To demonstrate the author's sense of humor

6. The author uses statistics to support the claim that recycling rates have increased significantly in recent years.

The main purpose of including statistics is to:

(A) Diminish the importance of recycling

(B) Provide evidence to support a key argument

(C) Challenge the idea that recycling has any benefits

(D) Argue that statistics are misleading

7. The passage follows a problem-solution format, detailing challenges faced by endangered species and proposing conservation methods.

What is the structure's purpose in this passage?

(A) To entertain readers with wildlife stories

(B) To persuade readers to donate to conservation efforts

(C) To inform readers about conservation issues and solutions

(D) To critique unsuccessful conservation methods

8. The writer discusses the historical context of a policy, highlighting its lasting impact on modern society.

The purpose of referencing historical context is to:

(A) Undermine the policy's current relevance

(B) Emphasize the policy's influence over time

(C) Challenge the legitimacy of the policy

(D) Introduce unrelated historical events

9. The author uses vivid imagery to describe the landscape, immersing the reader in the natural beauty of the region.

The use of vivid imagery serves to:

(A) Convince readers to visit the region

(B) Provide a factual description of the landscape

(C) Make the text more engaging and immersive

(D) Undermine the appeal of the region

10. The passage describes an experiment, listing the materials used, steps taken, and the results observed.

What is the purpose of this structure?

(A) To criticize the experiment's flaws

(B) To provide a clear, step-by-step explanation of the experiment

(C) To entertain readers with a humorous experiment

(D) To show the complexity of scientific studies

11. The author presents various viewpoints on climate change, ultimately arguing that urgent action is necessary.

What is the author's main purpose in presenting multiple viewpoints?

(A) To show indecision about climate change

(B) To provide balanced evidence before advocating for action

(C) To critique those who disagree with climate action

(D) To confuse the reader about the topic

12. The passage opens with a historical overview, then shifts to current events, linking past and present perspectives.

What is the function of this structure?

(A) To dismiss the relevance of history

(B) To highlight how history impacts current events

(C) To question the validity of modern ideas

(D) To portray a future-oriented perspective

13. The author's tone is satirical, using irony to criticize current social norms.

The purpose of using satire in this passage is to:

(A) Encourage readers to embrace the norms

(B) Make a humorous but critical commentary

(C) Provide an objective analysis

(D) Promote traditional values

14. The writer discusses the economic impact of renewable energy, focusing on potential job creation and costs.

What is the primary structure of this passage?

(A) Problem-solution

(B) Cause-effect

(C) Compare-contrast

(D) Process-analysis

15. In this passage, the writer introduces a hypothetical situation to illustrate a point about ethics.

The purpose of using a hypothetical example is to:

(A) Provide factual evidence

(B) Help readers visualize an abstract idea

(C) Confuse readers about ethical choices

(D) Undermine the ethical argument

16. The author uses a quote from a historical figure to strengthen their argument on individual rights.

Why does the author include this quote?

(A) To contradict the argument on individual rights

(B) To enhance credibility and support their stance

(C) To question the authority of historical figures

(D) To demonstrate a lack of evidence

17. The article includes a detailed comparison between fossil fuels and alternative energy sources, showing the advantages of both.

What is the main structure used here?

(A) Chronological order

(B) Cause-effect

(C) Compare-contrast

(D) Definition-example

18. The author ends with a call to action, urging readers to participate in community initiatives.

What is the purpose of this conclusion?

(A) To entertain readers with humor

(B) To challenge readers to think independently

(C) To inspire readers to take specific action

(D) To summarize earlier points

19. The author uses an analogy to explain complex scientific concepts, making them accessible to a general audience.

The primary purpose of using an analogy here is to:

(A) Simplify difficult concepts for readers

(B) Impress readers with scientific knowledge

(C) Undermine the complexity of the topic

(D) Argue against scientific explanations

20. The writer organizes the text by listing pros and cons, leading readers through a balanced exploration of the topic.

What is the main structure of this passage?

(A) Problem-solution

(B) Cause-effect

(C) Argument-counterargument

(D) Chronological

21. In the passage, the author draws on personal experience to illustrate a broader social issue.

Why might the author use personal experience?

(A) To enhance the objectivity of the argument

(B) To make the issue relatable for readers

(C) To undermine the significance of the issue

(D) To challenge readers' personal beliefs

22. The author uses data from recent studies to reinforce the argument about public health.

The primary purpose of including recent studies is to:

(A) Undermine public health arguments

(B) Offer reliable, updated support for the claim

(C) Question the validity of health data

(D) Disprove earlier research findings

23. The passage describes the various stages of a plant's growth cycle, from seed germination to flowering.

The structure of this passage can best be described as:

(A) Chronological order

(B) Cause-effect

(C) Compare-contrast

(D) Argument-counterargument

24. The author uses rhetorical questions to engage readers and provoke thought about environmental conservation.

What is the purpose of these rhetorical questions?

(A) To confuse the reader

(B) To engage readers and prompt reflection

(C) To make light of conservation efforts

(D) To dismiss environmental issues

25. The writer presents scientific theories alongside personal beliefs, showing where they align and diverge.

What is the primary structure used?

(A) Cause-effect

(B) Compare-contrast

(C) Argument-counterargument

(D) Chronological

26. The author starts with a bold claim, gradually providing supporting evidence throughout the passage.

What is the purpose of this structure?

(A) To disprove the initial claim

(B) To emphasize the claim through evidence

(C) To distract from the main argument

(D) To add humor to the claim

27. In the article, the author discusses both risks and rewards associated with investment strategies.

What is the main structure here?

(A) Problem-solution

(B) Cause-effect

(C) Compare-contrast

(D) Chronological order

28. The writer explains how the education system has evolved, highlighting major reforms over the decades.

What structure does the writer use?

(A) Argument-counterargument

(B) Chronological order

(C) Definition-example

(D) Cause-effect

29. The author ends by summarizing the key points and offering a reflective question for readers to consider.

What is the purpose of this conclusion?

(A) To offer new evidence

(B) To summarize and provoke thought

(C) To dismiss previous points

(D) To create suspense

30. The writer discusses the influence of art on culture, using specific examples from various art forms.

The primary purpose of using examples is to:

(A) Question the influence of art

(B) Undermine traditional art forms

(C) Illustrate the impact of art on society

(D) Provide evidence against art's relevance

Answer Explanations

1. (B) To describe the process and elements involved in coastal erosion – The sentence's focus is to explain the factors affecting erosion.

2. (C) To illustrate the speaker's effective communication style – The sentence emphasizes the scientist's clear and accessible presentation.

3. (B) The writer highlights complex problems with urban growth – The sentence introduces urban issues through a questioning approach.

4. (C) Contrast the challenges faced by each group – The comparison points out the varying experiences and obstacles of explorers and travelers.

5. (C) To engage readers before discussing complex topics – The anecdote serves to ease readers into the main discussion.

6. (B) Provide evidence to support a key argument – Statistics are used to reinforce the claim regarding recycling rates.

7. (C) To inform readers about conservation issues and solutions – The structure presents both problems and solutions, suitable for an informative tone.

8. (B) Emphasize the policy's influence over time – The historical context is referenced to underscore the policy's long-term impact.

9. (C) Make the text more engaging and immersive – Imagery adds a sensory dimension, helping readers visualize the landscape.

10. (B) To provide a clear, step-by-step explanation of the experiment – The structure of the passage is instructional, guiding readers through each phase of the experiment.

11. (B) To provide balanced evidence before advocating for action – The author builds a case by presenting multiple perspectives before promoting action.

12. (B) To highlight how history impacts current events – The structure connects historical events to current issues.

13. (B) Make a humorous but critical commentary – Satire and irony are used to critique social norms, not embrace them.

14. (B) Cause-effect – The passage links renewable energy use to economic impacts like job creation.

15. (B) Help readers visualize an abstract idea – Hypothetical scenarios can clarify complex ethical concepts.

16. (B) To enhance credibility and support their stance – Citing a historical figure strengthens the author's argument.

17. (C) Compare-contrast – The passage evaluates both fossil fuels and alternative energy sources.

18. (C) To inspire readers to take specific action – A call to action aims to motivate readers toward community engagement.

19. (A) Simplify difficult concepts for readers – Analogies help make complex scientific ideas more accessible.

20. (C) Argument-counterargument – Listing pros and cons leads to a balanced discussion of the topic.

21. (B) To make the issue relatable for readers – Personal experience can make broader social issues feel more tangible.

22. (B) Offer reliable, updated support for the claim – Recent studies enhance the validity of health-related arguments.

23. (A) Chronological order – The description follows the plant's growth from beginning to end.

24. (B) To engage readers and prompt reflection – Rhetorical questions encourage readers to think deeply.

25. (B) Compare-contrast – Scientific theories are compared and contrasted with personal beliefs.

26. (B) To emphasize the claim through evidence – The structure supports the initial claim by gradually adding evidence.

27. (C) Compare-contrast – Risks and rewards are contrasted to provide a balanced perspective on investment.

28. (B) Chronological order – The passage traces changes in education over time.

29. (B) To summarize and provoke thought – The conclusion recaps key points and leaves readers with a question to consider.

30. (C) Illustrate the impact of art on society – Examples from art highlight its influence on culture.

Cross-Text Connections

In the SAT Reading and Writing section, "Cross-Text Connections" questions challenge you to analyze the relationship between two different texts. This skill involves comparing themes, arguments, perspectives, and supporting details across multiple texts to see how they complement, contrast, or expand upon each other. By connecting the ideas and evidence presented in each text, you can better understand each author's purpose and the nuances in their points of view.

Key strategies for approaching Cross-Text Connections include:

- **Identifying Common Themes or Issues**: Recognize shared topics, such as environmental impact, historical events, or scientific advancements.
- **Evaluating Different Perspectives**: Pay attention to whether the authors agree, disagree, or offer distinct yet related insights on the same topic.
- **Understanding Supporting Details and Evidence**: See how each text uses examples or evidence to support its stance and look for instances where one text may build upon or contradict the other.

Mastering Cross-Text Connections will enhance your critical reading skills, helping you draw well-rounded conclusions from multiple sources. Now, let's dive into some practice questions to build this skill further.

Questions

1. Text 1 describes an author's nostalgic views on rural life, while Text 2 offers a critical perspective on urban expansion.

In what way are Text 1 and Text 2 connected?

(A) They both promote the benefits of urban life.

(B) They provide contrasting perspectives on rural and urban environments.

(C) They argue that rural areas should be preserved at all costs.

(D) They both support rapid urban development.

2. Text 1 discusses the ecological effects of deforestation. Text 2 presents an argument for preserving rainforests for biodiversity.

How does Text 2 build upon the ideas in Text 1?

(A) By explaining the economic benefits of deforestation

(B) By emphasizing the ecological necessity of biodiversity

(C) By arguing against any human intervention in rainforests

(D) By discussing urban areas affected by deforestation

3. Text 1 is about historical methods of irrigation, while Text 2 focuses on modern-day water conservation technologies.

What is a shared theme between Text 1 and Text 2?

(A) The environmental impacts of over-irrigation

(B) Advances in water usage efficiency over time

(C) The high costs of water conservation

(D) Diminishing water sources in arid regions

4. Text 1 outlines the scientific achievements of a renowned physicist, and Text 2 provides a summary of the physicist's philosophical views.

How does Text 2 add context to the information provided in Text 1?

(A) By introducing the physicist's personal life

(B) By showing how their scientific work influenced their philosophy

(C) By arguing against the physicist's theories

(D) By explaining the physicist's early career struggles

5. Text 1 highlights the challenges of maintaining a balanced diet, while Text 2 discusses the benefits of mindful eating.

What is a common purpose shared by both texts?

(A) To advocate for strict dietary restrictions

(B) To emphasize the importance of healthy eating habits

(C) To suggest that diet has little impact on health

(D) To recommend eliminating specific foods from one's diet

6. Text 1 discusses the importance of animal migration patterns, while Text 2 explains how climate change is altering these patterns.

How does Text 2 expand on the ideas in Text 1?

(A) By describing the benefits of climate change on migration

(B) By showing how migration patterns have become unpredictable

(C) By focusing on species that do not migrate

(D) By arguing that animal migration is not important

7. Text 1 provides a biographical account of an artist's early life. Text 2 explores the artist's impact on modern art.

What relationship does Text 2 have to Text 1?

(A) It contrasts with the artist's childhood struggles

(B) It connects the artist's early life to their artistic legacy

(C) It argues that the artist's work is overrated

(D) It focuses on art techniques unrelated to the artist

8. Text 1 explores the social benefits of sports for youth, while Text 2 highlights the psychological impact of competitive sports.

What common theme is shared by both texts?

(A) The need for more recreational facilities

(B) The impact of sports on youth development

(C) The risks of playing competitive sports

(D) The importance of winning in sports

9. Text 1 discusses the process of photosynthesis, while Text 2 explains its role in the ecosystem.

What is the relationship between Text 1 and Text 2?

(A) Text 2 critiques the process explained in Text 1

(B) Text 2 provides context for the importance of Text 1's topic

(C) Text 2 is unrelated to the concept of photosynthesis

(D) Text 2 focuses on photosynthesis in animals

10. Text 1 explains how social media influences consumer behavior, and Text 2 describes the rise of influencer marketing.

How does Text 2 build upon Text 1's discussion?

(A) By arguing against the effects of social media

(B) By providing a practical example of consumer influence

(C) By dismissing social media's role in marketing

(D) By explaining traditional forms of advertising

11. Text 1 describes the growth of urban farming, while Text 2 explains how it supports local economies.

How are the themes in Text 1 and Text 2 connected?

(A) Both discuss the challenges of rural farming

(B) Both examine the economic impact of urban farming

(C) Both focus on environmental issues

(D) Both emphasize health benefits

12. Text 1 presents the case for reducing plastic use, while Text 2 focuses on alternatives to plastic.

What relationship does Text 2 have to Text 1?

(A) Text 2 provides solutions to the issues raised in Text 1

(B) Text 2 challenges the argument in Text 1

(C) Text 2 suggests using more plastic

(D) Text 2 dismisses the environmental impact of plastic

13. Text 1 provides an overview of renewable energy sources, while Text 2 discusses the challenges of implementing these sources.

How does Text 2 relate to Text 1?

(A) By opposing the use of renewable energy

(B) By discussing the practical obstacles involved

(C) By introducing a new source of energy

(D) By celebrating the benefits of fossil fuels

14. Text 1 describes the lifestyle of early nomadic societies, and Text 2 discusses the shift to settled agricultural communities.

How do Text 1 and Text 2 connect?

(A) They describe unrelated historical events

(B) Text 2 explains a transition described in Text 1

(C) Text 1 critiques the lifestyle of agricultural societies

(D) Text 2 praises modern technology

15. Text 1 discusses the historical development of the printing press, while Text 2 examines its influence on literacy rates.

How does Text 2 expand on Text 1's ideas?

(A) By introducing challenges of the printing press

(B) By detailing the societal impact of the printing press

(C) By criticizing the effects of mass literacy

(D) By describing unrelated technological advances

16. Text 1 argues for the use of public transportation to reduce traffic congestion. Text 2 provides data on cities where this approach was successful.

How does Text 2 support Text 1?

(A) By suggesting alternatives to public transportation

(B) By offering evidence to back up Text 1's claim

(C) By showing that public transportation increases traffic

(D) By challenging the importance of reducing congestion

17. Text 1 explains the basic principles of classical architecture, while Text 2 illustrates how modern architects draw inspiration from it.

What connection is made between Text 1 and Text 2?

(A) They critique the appeal of classical architecture

(B) They show the influence of classical designs on modern structures

(C) They advocate for demolishing classical buildings

(D) They examine different styles unrelated to each other

18. Text 1 describes the role of women in ancient societies, while Text 2 compares it to women's roles in modern cultures.

How are Text 1 and Text 2 related?

(A) They contrast historical and contemporary roles of women

(B) They argue that women's roles have not changed

(C) They focus on one specific ancient society

(D) They describe the lack of change in women's rights

19. Text 1 describes the benefits of organic farming, while Text 2 discusses its environmental impact.

What common theme is shared between Text 1 and Text 2?

(A) The economic costs of organic farming

(B) The advantages of organic farming practices

(C) The reduced environmental impact of organic farming

(D) The challenges of switching to organic methods

20. Text 1 discusses the rise of electric vehicles, while Text 2 describes the impact of these vehicles on air quality.

How does Text 2 build on Text 1?

(A) By discussing economic incentives for electric vehicles

(B) By highlighting environmental benefits of electric vehicles

(C) By suggesting that electric vehicles are unnecessary

(D) By focusing on unrelated automotive technology

21. Text 1 introduces the concept of artificial intelligence, and Text 2 explores ethical concerns related to AI.

How are Text 1 and Text 2 connected?

(A) Text 2 provides a critical view on Text 1's subject

(B) Text 1 challenges the ethical concerns raised in Text 2

(C) Text 2 dismisses the importance of artificial intelligence

(D) Text 1 ignores ethical implications

22. Text 1 describes the process of urbanization, while Text 2 explores the impact of urban growth on natural habitats.

What relationship does Text 2 have with Text 1?

(A) Text 2 discusses the environmental consequences of urbanization

(B) Text 2 supports the rapid growth of urban areas

(C) Text 2 focuses on rural communities

(D) Text 2 argues against any form of urban development

23. Text 1 examines how students benefit from extracurricular activities. Text 2 discusses how involvement in these activities prepares students for future careers.

What shared purpose do both texts have?

(A) To advocate for increased funding for activities

(B) To emphasize the value of extracurricular engagement

(C) To suggest that activities have minimal benefits

(D) To focus solely on athletic programs

24. Text 1 explains the greenhouse effect, and Text 2 provides an example of how it affects specific ecosystems.

How does Text 2 support the ideas in Text 1?

(A) By focusing on solutions to climate change

(B) By offering a practical example of the greenhouse effect

(C) By discussing unrelated environmental concepts

(D) By arguing against the greenhouse effect

25. Text 1 describes techniques for effective time management, while Text 2 illustrates how these techniques can reduce stress.

What connection does Text 2 have to Text 1?

(A) It criticizes time management strategies

(B) It explains the benefits of applying these strategies

(C) It suggests time management is unnecessary

(D) It describes a different approach unrelated to time management

26. Text 1 provides an overview of renewable energy sources, while Text 2 explores specific policies for implementing these sources.

How does Text 2 build on Text 1?

(A) By opposing renewable energy policies

(B) By discussing practical applications of the concepts in Text 1

(C) By introducing a new form of energy

(D) By focusing only on fossil fuels

27. Text 1 describes characteristics of various literary genres, while Text 2 discusses how genres have evolved over time.

What relationship does Text 2 have to Text 1?

(A) It provides historical context to complement Text 1

(B) It argues for one genre over another

(C) It presents genres not discussed in Text 1

(D) It dismisses the importance of literary genres

28. Text 1 examines traditional farming practices, while Text 2 explains innovations that have transformed agriculture in recent years.

How does Text 2 relate to Text 1?

(A) By opposing the use of traditional methods

(B) By illustrating modern advancements that expand on Text 1

(C) By arguing against agricultural innovation

(D) By focusing only on subsistence farming

29. Text 1 highlights the role of space exploration in technological advances, while Text 2 debates the ethical implications of space colonization.

What is a shared theme between Text 1 and Text 2?

(A) The scientific achievements of space travel

(B) Ethical concerns surrounding scientific exploration

(C) Reasons for halting space exploration

(D) The lack of necessity for space programs

30. Text 1 explains the fundamentals of economic supply and demand, while Text 2 uses a case study to illustrate these principles in action.

How does Text 2 build on the ideas introduced in Text 1?

(A) By introducing unrelated economic concepts

(B) By providing a practical example to support Text 1's theory

(C) By questioning the principles of supply and demand

(D) By discussing non-economic factors

Answer Explanations

1. (B) They provide contrasting perspectives on rural and urban environments – Text 1 is nostalgic for rural life, while Text 2 critically examines urban expansion, providing a balanced perspective through contrast.

2. (B) By emphasizing the ecological necessity of biodiversity – Text 2 builds on the ecological discussion in Text 1 by focusing on biodiversity, reinforcing the importance of rainforests for maintaining ecological balance.

3. (B) Advances in water usage efficiency over time – Both texts share a focus on water management, with Text 1 covering historical irrigation and Text 2 detailing modern conservation methods.

4. (B) By showing how their scientific work influenced their philosophy – Text 2 provides insight into how the physicist's achievements impacted their worldview, adding depth to the achievements listed in Text 1.

5. (B) To emphasize the importance of healthy eating habits – Both texts discuss aspects of nutrition aimed at promoting a healthier lifestyle, making this a shared purpose.

6. (B) By showing how migration patterns have become unpredictable – Text 2 builds on Text 1 by addressing how climate change disrupts migration, adding a new perspective.

7. (B) It connects the artist's early life to their artistic legacy – Text 2 examines the impact of the artist's early experiences, adding context to Text 1.

8. (B) The impact of sports on youth development – Both texts examine how sports contribute to different aspects of youth growth.

9. (B) Text 2 provides context for the importance of Text 1's topic – Text 2 explains why photosynthesis is significant in ecosystems, complementing the scientific explanation in Text 1.

10. (B) By providing a practical example of consumer influence – Text 2 expands on social media's impact by discussing influencer marketing, a real-world application.

11. (B) Both examine the economic impact of urban farming – Both texts focus on how urban farming contributes to the economy.

12. (A) Text 2 provides solutions to the issues raised in Text 1 – Text 2 suggests alternatives that help address the plastic issues mentioned in Text 1.

13. (B) By discussing the practical obstacles involved – Text 2 explores challenges related to implementing renewable energy, adding depth to Text 1's overview.

14. (B) Text 2 explains a transition described in Text 1 – Text 2 describes the shift from nomadic to settled communities.

15. (B) By detailing the societal impact of the printing press – Text 2 expands on Text 1's historical focus by discussing how the printing press influenced society.

16. (B) By offering evidence to back up Text 1's claim – Text 2 provides specific examples of successful public transportation use, reinforcing Text 1's argument.

17. (B) They show the influence of classical designs on modern structures – Text 2 examines how modern architects draw from classical styles.

18. (A) They contrast historical and contemporary roles of women – Both texts discuss women's roles, with Text 2 contrasting them against modern norms.

19. (C) The reduced environmental impact of organic farming – Both texts discuss the benefits of organic farming on the environment.

20. (B) By highlighting environmental benefits of electric vehicles – Text 2 discusses how electric vehicles positively impact air quality, supporting Text 1.

21. (A) Text 2 provides a critical view on Text 1's subject – Text 1 introduces AI, while Text 2 adds a critical lens by examining ethical concerns, thus expanding the discussion introduced in Text 1.

22. (A) Text 2 discusses the environmental consequences of urbanization – Text 2 builds on the topic of urbanization from Text 1 by specifically addressing its impact on natural habitats.

23. (B) To emphasize the value of extracurricular engagement – Both texts highlight different benefits of extracurricular activities, from personal growth to career preparation, underscoring their value.

24. (B) By offering a practical example of the greenhouse effect – Text 2 supports the scientific explanation in Text 1 by showing how the greenhouse effect impacts real ecosystems.

25. (B) It explains the benefits of applying these strategies – Text 2 illustrates how the time management methods described in Text 1 can help reduce stress, adding practical applications to the strategies introduced.

26. (B) By discussing practical applications of the concepts in Text 1 – Text 2 builds upon the general information about renewable energy in Text 1 by exploring specific policies for implementation.

27. (A) It provides historical context to complement Text 1 – Text 2 discusses how literary genres have evolved over time, providing historical context for the genres described in Text 1.

28. (B) By illustrating modern advancements that expand on Text 1 – Text 2 focuses on innovations in agriculture, which serve as a modern extension of the traditional practices described in Text 1.

29. (B) Ethical concerns surrounding scientific exploration – Both texts discuss aspects of space exploration, with a shared theme that highlights potential ethical issues involved in scientific advancement.

30. (B) By providing a practical example to support Text 1's theory – Text 2 takes the theoretical concepts of supply and demand introduced in Text 1 and uses a case study to illustrate how these principles work in practice.

Central Ideas and Details

In the SAT Reading and Writing section, questions about "Central Ideas and Details" are designed to test your ability to identify an author's main point and understand how specific details support that point. Recognizing the central idea requires you to look beyond specific facts or examples and focus on the overarching message or argument that the author is conveying. Details, on the other hand, serve as supporting evidence, examples, or explanations that reinforce and clarify the main idea.

Key strategies for these questions include:

- **Identifying Topic Sentences**: Often, the first or last sentence of a paragraph provides insight into its central idea.
- **Summarizing Key Details**: Highlight details that explain, reinforce, or illustrate the main idea.
- **Distinguishing Main Ideas from Minor Details**: Focus on the most important points while recognizing which parts are secondary.

Mastering this skill will enhance your comprehension of complex texts and help you efficiently extract meaning, especially when faced with time constraints. Now, let's dive into practice questions to further develop this skill!

Questions

1. The author explains the long-term consequences of climate change on polar habitats, emphasizing the loss of biodiversity.

What is the main idea of this sentence?

(A) Climate change has minimal impact on polar regions.

(B) Climate change will have a major effect on biodiversity in polar regions.

(C) Biodiversity in polar regions is increasing.

(D) Polar habitats are unaffected by climate change.

2. The text describes how community gardens can help urban residents access fresh produce and promote environmental awareness.

What is the central idea of this passage?

(A) Community gardens are costly to maintain.

(B) Community gardens improve access to fresh food and promote environmental education.

(C) Urban residents are uninterested in gardening.

(D) Only children benefit from community gardens.

3. The passage highlights the rapid development of renewable energy technologies and discusses the challenges these innovations face.

What is the primary purpose of this passage?

(A) To discourage the use of renewable energy

(B) To celebrate the achievements of renewable energy

(C) To present the growth and obstacles of renewable energy technologies

(D) To argue that renewable energy is ineffective

4. The author describes how artificial intelligence can automate certain tasks, leading to increased efficiency in various industries.

What is the main idea of the passage?

(A) AI reduces jobs in all industries.

(B) AI can help increase productivity by automating tasks.

(C) AI is irrelevant to industrial productivity.

(D) AI is too complex to be widely implemented.

5. The passage compares two approaches to wildlife conservation, highlighting the benefits and drawbacks of each.

What is the purpose of comparing these approaches?

(A) To prove one approach is superior

(B) To showcase the pros and cons of different conservation methods

(C) To argue against wildlife conservation

(D) To describe the cost of conservation efforts

6. The author discusses the effects of pollution on marine life, emphasizing the need for stricter regulations.

What is the central idea of this passage?

(A) Marine life is unaffected by pollution.

(B) Pollution is harming marine ecosystems, and stricter rules are needed.

(C) Regulations on marine pollution are unnecessary.

(D) The author discusses various benefits of pollution.

7. The text details how a balanced diet can improve mental clarity and physical well-being.

What is the main idea?

(A) Diet has little effect on health.

(B) Proper nutrition positively impacts both mental and physical health.

(C) Physical well-being is unrelated to diet.

(D) Balanced diets are too difficult to follow.

8. The passage explores how certain plant species adapt to extreme climates, such as deserts and tundras.

What is the central idea of this passage?

(A) Plants cannot survive in extreme climates.

(B) Some plants have unique adaptations for survival in harsh environments.

(C) Only desert plants can adapt to extreme climates.

(D) Extreme climates support limited vegetation.

9. The author explains the benefits of renewable energy, particularly solar and wind power, for reducing carbon emissions.

What is the main idea of this passage?

(A) Renewable energy increases carbon emissions.

(B) Solar and wind energy have no impact on the environment.

(C) Renewable energy helps lower carbon emissions.

(D) Only solar energy is beneficial.

10. The passage illustrates the rise of digital media and its impact on traditional print industries.

What is the primary purpose of this passage?

(A) To argue that print media is obsolete

(B) To explore how digital media is changing print industries

(C) To support the return of print media

(D) To critique digital media for being ineffective

11. The author discusses the history of the Great Wall of China, focusing on its construction and cultural significance.

What is the central idea?

(A) The Great Wall has little historical importance.

(B) The Great Wall is an important cultural and historical landmark.

(C) The Great Wall was never completed.

(D) The Great Wall was built for aesthetic reasons only.

12. The passage highlights the role of parents in children's education, emphasizing communication and support.

What is the main idea?

(A) Parents should not interfere in their children's education.

(B) Parental involvement, communication, and support are key to a child's education.

(C) Education should be entirely school-based.

(D) Children do not benefit from parental involvement in education.

13. The text explains how bees play a critical role in pollinating crops, which helps sustain agricultural productivity.

What is the main idea?

(A) Bees have minimal impact on agriculture.

(B) Bees are essential to crop pollination and agricultural success.

(C) Crop pollination is primarily handled by wind.

(D) Bees are only beneficial to wild plants.

14. The passage compares traditional farming techniques to modern agricultural practices, discussing the pros and cons of each.

What is the purpose of comparing these farming methods?

(A) To prove that modern methods are superior

(B) To objectively present the strengths and weaknesses of both techniques

(C) To advocate for traditional farming only

(D) To highlight the inefficiency of both methods

15. The author describes the importance of biodiversity in maintaining a balanced ecosystem.

What is the central idea?

(A) Biodiversity has little impact on ecosystems.

(B) Biodiversity is crucial for ecosystem stability.

(C) Balanced ecosystems require minimal biodiversity.

(D) Biodiversity only affects tropical regions.

16. The text discusses the history and impact of the printing press on literacy and education.

What is the main idea?

(A) The printing press had a negligible effect on education.

(B) The printing press revolutionized literacy and access to education.

(C) Education and literacy existed in limited forms before the printing press.

(D) The printing press was only used for newspapers.

17. The passage outlines the process of photosynthesis and its significance in the food chain.

What is the primary purpose of this passage?

(A) To explore photosynthesis as irrelevant

(B) To describe the photosynthesis process and its role in the ecosystem

(C) To argue against the necessity of photosynthesis

(D) To introduce alternatives to photosynthesis

18. The author explains how exercise can improve both physical and mental health, providing specific examples.

What is the main idea?

(A) Exercise has little effect on health.

(B) Exercise benefits physical health but not mental health.

(C) Physical and mental health can both improve with regular exercise.

(D) Only mental health benefits from exercise.

19. The text explores the global efforts to combat climate change, focusing on policy and individual actions.

What is the central idea?

(A) Climate change requires only policy changes.

(B) Both policy and individual actions play a role in addressing climate change.

(C) Individual actions are irrelevant to climate change.

(D) Only corporations can combat climate change.

20. The passage describes various educational reforms and their impact on student performance.

What is the main idea?

(A) Educational reforms have no effect on students.

(B) Recent reforms aim to enhance student learning and outcomes.

(C) Education is unaffected by policy changes.

(D) Reforms are needed but have been ineffective.

21. The author discusses the benefits of traveling internationally and how it can foster cultural understanding.

What is the primary purpose?

(A) To discourage international travel

(B) To highlight how travel promotes cultural awareness

(C) To focus on the economic costs of travel

(D) To argue for stricter travel regulations

22. The text discusses renewable resources and why they are essential for a sustainable future.

What is the main idea?

(A) Renewable resources are unimportant for sustainability.

(B) Renewable resources play a critical role in sustainable development.

(C) Only non-renewable resources are essential.

(D) Sustainable futures do not depend on resource types.

23. The passage illustrates how teamwork and collaboration can lead to more effective problem-solving.

What is the central idea?

(A) Teamwork has little impact on problem-solving.

(B) Working together can enhance the ability to solve complex problems.

(C) Problem-solving is best done alone.

(D) Collaboration hinders effective solutions.

24. The author explains how technological advancements have changed the way people communicate, focusing on social media and instant messaging.

What is the main idea?

(A) Technology has minimal effect on communication.

(B) New technology has transformed interpersonal communication.

(C) Instant messaging is outdated.

(D) Social media is the only technological advancement discussed.

25. The passage explores different perspectives on artificial intelligence and its future implications.

What is the primary purpose?

(A) To provide a balanced view on AI and its potential impacts

(B) To argue against the development of AI

(C) To show that AI has no future use

(D) To describe how AI will replace all jobs

26. The text explains how natural disasters impact communities and discusses measures to enhance resilience.

What is the main idea?

(A) Natural disasters have minimal impact on communities.

(B) Communities must build resilience to withstand natural disasters.

(C) Natural disasters are beneficial.

(D) Resilience is irrelevant to disaster management.

27. The author describes how childhood experiences can shape an individual's personality and behavior.

What is the central idea?

(A) Childhood has little influence on adult behavior.

(B) Early experiences play a role in personal development.

(C) Personality is unchanging from birth.

(D) Personality is unaffected by experiences.

28. The passage highlights the importance of creative thinking in solving complex problems.

What is the main idea?

(A) Creativity has no role in problem-solving.

(B) Creative approaches can aid in addressing difficult challenges.

(C) Simple solutions are always best.

(D) Problem-solving only requires logic.

29. The text discusses the role of music in cultural expression and its power to connect communities.

What is the primary purpose?

(A) To suggest that music is divisive

(B) To illustrate music's role in fostering cultural unity

(C) To argue that music is outdated

(D) To describe musical trends

30. The author examines how technology in medicine has improved patient outcomes and increased life expectancy.

What is the central idea?

(A) Medical technology has little effect on health.

(B) Advances in technology have enhanced patient outcomes and increased life expectancy

Answer Explanations

1. (B) Climate change will have a major effect on biodiversity in polar regions – The passage clearly discusses the impact of climate change on polar biodiversity.

2. (B) Community gardens improve access to fresh food and promote environmental education – The passage highlights the benefits of community gardens, making this the main idea.

3. (C) To present the growth and obstacles of renewable energy technologies – The passage aims to describe both the achievements and challenges of renewable energy.

4. (B) AI can help increase productivity by automating tasks – This is the main idea, as the passage focuses on AI's role in increasing efficiency.

5. (B) To showcase the pros and cons of different conservation methods – The purpose is to objectively compare different conservation approaches.

6. (B) Pollution is harming marine ecosystems, and stricter rules are needed – The passage's focus is on pollution's negative effects on marine life, with a clear call for stronger regulations to protect these environments, making option (B) the best choice.

7. (B) Proper nutrition positively impacts both mental and physical health – This option captures the main idea that a balanced diet contributes to both mental clarity and physical wellness, aligning with the passage's emphasis.

8. (B) Some plants have unique adaptations for survival in harsh environments – This choice reflects the main point that certain plants adapt to extreme climates like deserts and tundras, making (B) the correct answer.

9. (C) Renewable energy helps lower carbon emissions – The passage highlights how renewable sources, particularly solar and wind power, contribute to reducing emissions, clearly supporting (C) as the main idea.

10. (B) To explore how digital media is changing print industries – The passage examines the influence of digital media on traditional print industries, so (B) accurately captures the main idea, as it focuses on the transformation rather than obsolescence.

11. (B) The Great Wall is an important cultural and historical landmark – This option correctly summarizes the significance of the Great Wall of China in both historical and cultural terms, as discussed in the passage.

12. (B) Parental involvement, communication, and support are key to a child's education – The main idea emphasizes the positive impact of parental engagement in children's educational journeys, aligning with (B).

13. (B) Bees are essential to crop pollination and agricultural success – This answer highlights the critical role bees play in pollinating crops, which directly supports agricultural productivity, making (B) the central idea.

14. (B) To objectively present the strengths and weaknesses of both techniques – The passage's comparison of farming techniques is balanced, presenting both pros and cons without promoting one over the other, which makes (B) the best fit.

15. (B) Biodiversity is crucial for ecosystem stability – This option correctly identifies biodiversity as necessary for maintaining balanced ecosystems, matching the passage's central idea.

16. (B) The printing press revolutionized literacy and access to education – The passage's main point is the transformative effect of the printing press on literacy, supporting the idea of increased accessibility, which makes (B) correct.

17. (B) To describe the photosynthesis process and its role in the ecosystem – The passage focuses on explaining photosynthesis and its importance in the food chain, making (B) the main purpose.

18. (C) Physical and mental health can both improve with regular exercise – The author highlights how exercise benefits both types of health, so (C) captures the complete main idea.

19. (B) Both policy and individual actions play a role in addressing climate change – This option accurately reflects the passage's main idea by acknowledging the combined efforts of policy and individual contributions in combating climate change.

20. (B) Recent reforms aim to enhance student learning and outcomes – The main idea focuses on how educational reforms are implemented to improve student performance, making (B) the correct answer.

21. (B) To highlight how travel promotes cultural awareness – The passage emphasizes international travel as a way to foster cultural understanding, so (B) reflects the primary purpose.

22. (B) Renewable resources play a critical role in sustainable development – This option aligns with the passage's focus on renewable resources being essential for a sustainable future, making (B) the correct answer.

23. (B) Working together can enhance the ability to solve complex problems – This option captures the main idea that teamwork improves problem-solving, which is the primary point of the passage.

24. (B) New technology has transformed interpersonal communication – The passage discusses how social media and instant messaging have reshaped communication, making (B) the main idea.

25. (A) To provide a balanced view on AI and its potential impacts – This choice accurately represents the passage's exploration of various perspectives on AI, emphasizing a balanced viewpoint.

26. (B) Communities must build resilience to withstand natural disasters – The main idea stresses the importance of resilience for communities facing natural disasters, making (B) the best option.

27. (B) Early experiences play a role in personal development – This choice correctly identifies childhood experiences as influential in shaping personality and behavior, aligning with the main idea.

28. (B) Creative approaches can aid in addressing difficult challenges – This option captures the passage's emphasis on creative thinking as a valuable tool for problem-solving, making (B) the best fit.

29. (B) To illustrate music's role in fostering cultural unity – The main purpose of the passage is to show how music brings communities together and reflects cultural expression, making (B) the correct answer.

30. (B) Advances in technology have enhanced patient outcomes and increased life expectancy – The passage highlights how technology in medicine has positively impacted health, making (B) the best choice for the central idea.

Quantitative Evidence

In the SAT Reading and Writing section, "Quantitative Evidence" questions evaluate your ability to interpret and analyze numerical data within a text. These questions require you to combine reading skills with quantitative reasoning to understand how specific figures, percentages, or proportions support or clarify an author's argument. Quantitative evidence can appear in the form of percentages, statistical comparisons, data trends, or other numerical details embedded in the passage.

Key strategies for answering quantitative evidence questions include:

- **Identifying Numerical Relationships**: Determine how numbers relate to one another in terms of increases, decreases, or proportions.
- **Interpreting Context**: Understand why the author includes certain data and what role it plays in supporting the main idea.
- **Calculating Percentages and Ratios**: Be comfortable with basic calculations, especially for percentages, as these are common in data interpretation questions.

By practicing quantitative reasoning alongside reading comprehension, you will build skills to efficiently interpret data, making you better prepared for complex, data-driven questions. Now, let's begin with some practice questions to strengthen this skill set!

Questions

1. A survey found that 55% of students prefer online learning, while 30% prefer in-person classes, and the remaining prefer a hybrid model.

What percentage of students prefer a hybrid model?

(A) 10%

(B) 15%

(C) 25%

(D) 30%

2. In a small town, there are 3,000 registered vehicles. Of these, 40% are electric vehicles.

How many electric vehicles are in the town?

(A) 800

(B) 1,000

(C) 1,200

(D) 1,500

3. A school has a total of 1,200 students, of whom 20% are enrolled in advanced science courses.

How many students are in advanced science courses?

(A) 180

(B) 200

(C) 240

(D) 300

4. An office has 150 employees, and 60% of them commute by public transportation.

How many employees commute by public transportation?

(A) 75

(B) 90

(C) 100

(D) 120

5. A poll showed that 65% of participants supported a proposed policy, while the rest opposed it.

If there were 800 participants, how many opposed the policy?

(A) 240

(B) 280

(C) 320

(D) 360

6. In a survey, 25% of respondents preferred reading over other leisure activities.

If there were 400 respondents, how many preferred reading?

(A) 50

(B) 75

(C) 100

(D) 125

7. In a high school, 30% of the 900 students participate in sports.

How many students participate in sports?

(A) 200

(B) 270

(C) 300

(D) 330

8. An organization found that 70% of its members volunteer regularly.

If the organization has 600 members, how many volunteer regularly?

(A) 300

(B) 400

(C) 420

(D) 450

9. A company allocates 15% of its budget to research and development.

If the company's total budget is \$2 million, how much is allocated to research and development?

(A) \$200,000

(B) \$250,000

(C) \$300,000

(D) \$350,000

10. In a test of 50 questions, a student answered 84% correctly.

How many questions did the student answer correctly?

(A) 40

(B) 42

(C) 44

(D) 46

11. A community center surveyed its visitors and found that 80% attend workshops regularly.

If there are 500 visitors, how many attend workshops?

(A) 300

(B) 350

(C) 400

(D) 450

12. A charity organization raised $1,500,000 and allocated 60% of it to its health programs.

How much was allocated to health programs?

(A) $750,000

(B) $850,000

(C) $900,000

(D) $950,000

13. In a city, 45% of households have recycling programs, while the rest do not.

If there are 12,000 households, how many do not recycle?

(A) 5,400

(B) 6,600

(C) 7,200

(D) 8,000

14. A factory increased its production by 25% this year compared to last year.

If last year's production was 1,200 units, what is this year's production?

(A) 1,300 units

(B) 1,400 units

(C) 1,500 units

(D) 1,600 units

15. A university has 10,000 students, and 65% receive some form of financial aid.

How many students receive financial aid?

(A) 5,500

(B) 6,000

(C) 6,500

(D) 7,000

16. A fitness club found that 75% of its members use the gym at least once a week.

If there are 400 members, how many use the gym weekly?

(A) 280

(B) 300

(C) 320

(D) 350

17. An online store reported that 30% of its monthly sales come from new customers.

If the store had 2,000 sales in a month, how many were from new customers?

(A) 500

(B) 600

(C) 700

(D) 800

18. A city's budget allocates 20% to public safety.

If the budget is $15 million, how much is allocated to public safety?

(A) $2 million

(B) $3 million

(C) $4 million

(D) $5 million

19. A company reduced its water usage by 40% over a year.

If it originally used 500,000 gallons, how much does it use now?

(A) 250,000 gallons

(B) 300,000 gallons

(C) 350,000 gallons

(D) 400,000 gallons

20. An organization found that 90% of its donors contribute annually.

If there are 800 donors, how many contribute each year?

(A) 640

(B) 700

(C) 720

(D) 760

21. A tech company devotes 45% of its workforce to research and development.

If it has 2,200 employees, how many work in R&D?

(A) 950

(B) 980

(C) 990

(D) 1,000

22. In a college class of 300 students, 55% passed their final exam on the first attempt.

How many students passed the exam?

(A) 150

(B) 165

(C) 180

(D) 200

23. A city's population grew by 12% over a decade.

If the population was 100,000, what is the new population?

(A) 110,000

(B) 111,000

(C) 112,000

(D) 113,000

24. A bank's customer survey revealed that 25% use online banking services exclusively.

If there are 10,000 customers, how many use only online banking?

(A) 2,000

(B) 2,500

(C) 3,000

(D) 3,500

25. A high school reported that 40% of its 1,500 students participate in extracurricular activities.

How many students participate?

(A) 500

(B) 600

(C) 700

(D) 750

26. A company reports that 80% of its new hires complete their training.

If there were 250 new hires, how many completed the training?

(A) 150

(B) 175

(C) 200

(D) 225

27. In a local election, 58% of 10,000 registered voters participated.

How many voters participated?

(A) 5,600

(B) 5,800

(C) 6,000

(D) 6,200

28. A nonprofit organization spends 30% of its $2 million budget on educational programs.

How much is allocated to educational programs?

(A) $500,000

(B) $600,000

(C) $700,000

(D) $800,000

29. A concert venue was 75% full with 3,000 attendees.

What is the venue's total capacity?

(A) 3,500

(B) 3,750

(C) 4,000

(D) 4,500

30. An agricultural study found that 15% of crops were lost to pests.

If the farm produced 20,000 units, how many units were lost?

(A) 2,000

(B) 2,500

(C) 3,000

(D) 3,500

Answer Explanations

1. (B) 15% – 55% prefer online, and 30% prefer in-person, totaling 85%. The remaining 15% prefer a hybrid model.

2. (C) 1,200 – 40% of 3,000 vehicles equals $0.4 \times 3000 = 1200$.

3. (C) 240 – 20% of 1,200 students is $0.2 \times 1200 = 240$.

4. (B) 90 – 60% of 150 employees is $0.6 \times 150 = 90$.

5. (C) 320 – 35% (100% - 65%) of 800 participants is $0.35 \times 800 = 320$.

6. (C) 100 – 25% of 400 respondents is $0.25 \times 400 = 100$.

7. (B) 270 – 30% of 900 students is $0.3 \times 900 = 270$.

8. (C) 420 – 70% of 600 members is $0.7 \times 600 = 420$.

9. (C) $300,000 – 15% of a $2 million budget is 0.15×2000000=300000.

10. (B) 42 – 84% of 50 questions is 0.84×50=42.

11. (D) 450 – 80% of 500 visitors is 0.8×500=450.

12. (C) $900,000 – 60% of $1,500,000 is 0.6×1500000=900000.

13. (B) 6,600 – 55% of 12,000 households do not recycle, or 0.55×12000=6600.

14. (C) 1,500 units – 25% of 1,200 units is an increase of 0.25×1200=300, making the new total 1200+300=1500.

15. (C) 6,500 – 65% of 10,000 students is 0.65×10000=6500.

16. (C) 320 – 75% of 400 members is 0.75×400=320.

17. (B) 600 – 30% of 2,000 sales is 0.3×2000=600.

18. (B) $3 million – 20% of $15 million is 0.2×15000000=3000000.

19. (B) 300,000 gallons – Reducing by 40% leaves 60%, so 0.6×500000=300000.

20. (C) 720 – 90% of 800 donors is 0.9×800=720.

21. (C) 990 – 45% of 2,200 employees is 0.45×2200=990.

22. (C) 180 – 55% of 300 students is 0.55×300=180.

23. (C) 112,000 – A 12% increase of 100,000 is 0.12×100000=12000, giving a new total of 100000+12000=112000.

24. (B) 2,500 – 25% of 10,000 customers is 0.25×10000=2500.

25. (D) 750 – 40% of 1,500 students is 0.4×1500=750.

26. (D) 225 – 80% of 250 hires is 0.8×250=225.

27. (B) 5,800 – 58% of 10,000 voters is 0.58×10000=5800.

28. (B) $600,000 – 30% of $2 million is calculated as 0.3×2000000=600000, so the correct answer is (B).

29. (C) 4,000 – If 75% occupancy is equal to 3,000 attendees, the total capacity is 3000 ÷ 0.75 = 4000.

30. (B) 3,000 – 15% of 20,000 units is 0.15×20000=3000, so (B) is the correct answer.

Textual Evidence

In the SAT Reading and Writing section, "Textual Evidence" questions require you to evaluate and interpret specific pieces of information within a passage to determine how well they support claims or arguments. This skill tests your ability to identify relevant details that reinforce the author's perspective or counter opposing viewpoints. In these questions, evidence can appear as specific facts, examples, statistics, or quotes that the author uses to validate their main idea or argument.

Strategies for answering textual evidence questions include:

- **Finding Directly Related Information**: Focus on locating specific details that directly relate to the claim or argument presented.
- **Evaluating Relevance and Support**: Determine if the information strongly supports or merely relates to the claim.
- **Recognizing Contradictions**: Be aware of evidence that may weaken or contradict a claim.

Developing this skill will help you analyze passages effectively, allowing you to draw well-founded conclusions based on the strength of the evidence. Now, let's dive into some practice questions to strengthen your understanding of textual evidence!

Questions

1. A journalist claims that pollution levels have decreased significantly in the last decade due to stricter regulations.

Which of the following, if true, would most directly support the journalist's claim?

(A) Emission records indicate a 40% decrease in pollutants over ten years.

(B) Citizens have been more vocal about environmental issues.

(C) Companies have increased their advertising about green practices.

(D) Fewer cases of respiratory illness have been reported recently.

2. A historian argues that women have consistently played critical roles in social reform movements.

Which of the following findings would most directly support this argument?

(A) Women often led key parts of the abolitionist movement.

(B) Social reforms were mainly driven by financial needs.

(C) Political reforms were mostly led by male figures.

(D) Educational programs in the 19th century often excluded women.

3. An economist claims that remote work will lead to economic benefits for small towns.

Which piece of evidence would best support this claim?

(A) The cost of living has decreased in urban areas.

(B) Many companies have adopted flexible work policies.

(C) Local businesses in small towns report revenue growth due to remote workers.

(D) Cities are creating new job opportunities.

4. A psychologist suggests that social media use correlates with lower levels of self-esteem among teenagers.

Which of the following, if true, would most directly support this suggestion?

(A) Teenagers report feeling less satisfied with their lives after using social media.

(B) Adults use social media differently than teenagers.

(C) Teenagers often use social media to connect with friends.

(D) Many teenagers prefer in-person interactions over social media.

5. A recent report indicates that hybrid cars reduce greenhouse gas emissions by a significant margin compared to conventional cars.

Which finding would best support the report's indication?

(A) Hybrid cars are more expensive than conventional cars.

(B) Studies show a 30% reduction in emissions from hybrid vehicles.

(C) Electric vehicles have no emissions at all.

(D) Hybrid cars are popular in urban areas.

6. A health report suggests that regular exercise can reduce the risk of chronic illnesses.

Which of the following pieces of evidence would best support this report?

(A) Patients who exercise regularly report feeling happier.

(B) Studies show a 40% reduction in chronic illness among regular exercisers.

(C) Exercising helps improve mental health.

(D) Regular exercise reduces the likelihood of injuries.

7. An environmentalist claims that deforestation directly impacts the availability of clean water.

Which piece of evidence would most directly support this claim?

(A) Forests help in water purification and maintaining watersheds.

(B) Clean water is essential for health.

(C) Deforestation also impacts biodiversity.

(D) Clean water is becoming scarce worldwide.

8. A sociologist argues that urbanization contributes to rising rates of mental health issues.

Which of the following, if true, would most strongly support the sociologist's argument?

(A) Mental health resources are often lacking in urban centers.

(B) Many urban residents report high stress levels.

(C) People often feel more isolated in crowded urban settings.

(D) More studies are needed to examine urbanization's impact on health.

9. A scientist proposes that introducing native plants into urban areas improves biodiversity.

Which piece of evidence would most support this proposal?

(A) Native plants adapt well to urban pollution levels.

(B) Native plants attract local wildlife, which supports ecosystem health.

(C) Most urban areas lack green spaces.

(D) Biodiversity is lower in cities than in rural areas.

10. An economist asserts that small businesses drive job creation in local economies.

Which piece of evidence would best support the economist's assertion?

(A) Many small businesses are family-owned.

(B) Statistics show that small businesses created 60% of new jobs in recent years.

(C) Small businesses struggle to compete with large corporations.

(D) Small businesses contribute significantly to tax revenue.

11. A climate scientist argues that rising global temperatures affect agricultural yields.

Which piece of evidence would best support this claim?

(A) Certain crops have become more difficult to grow in warm climates.

(B) Farmers have reported changes in seasonal patterns.

(C) Global temperatures have risen by 1 degree in the last century.

(D) Agricultural machinery has not adapted to climate change.

12. An educator claims that project-based learning improves student engagement.

Which of the following pieces of evidence would support this claim?

(A) Project-based learning helps develop teamwork skills.

(B) Students report feeling more involved in classes with hands-on projects.

(C) Teachers often find it challenging to design projects.

(D) Standardized test scores are unaffected by project-based learning.

13. A nutritionist asserts that diets high in fiber reduce the risk of heart disease.

Which piece of evidence would best support this assertion?

(A) Fiber is commonly found in vegetables and whole grains.

(B) Research shows that high-fiber diets are linked to a 30% lower risk of heart disease.

(C) People who eat more fiber tend to weigh less.

(D) Heart disease risk is influenced by many factors.

14. A wildlife researcher states that conservation areas help endangered species recover.

Which of the following findings would most strongly support this statement?

(A) Many endangered species live in isolated habitats.

(B) Conservation areas restrict human activities.

(C) Populations of endangered species have increased in protected areas.

(D) Species in conservation areas have limited genetic diversity.

15. A study claims that reading regularly can improve vocabulary skills.

Which of the following pieces of evidence best supports this claim?

(A) People who read frequently have larger vocabularies than non-readers.

(B) Reading can reduce stress levels.

(C) Vocabulary skills are essential in academic settings.

(D) Many readers enjoy fiction over nonfiction.

16. A business analyst suggests that employee satisfaction correlates with increased productivity.

What would most directly support this suggestion?

(A) Satisfied employees report fewer absences from work.

(B) Companies with high employee satisfaction see a 20% boost in productivity.

(C) Productivity can vary based on job type.

(D) Employee satisfaction is difficult to measure.

17. A doctor claims that smoking cessation significantly lowers the risk of lung disease.

Which of the following would best support this claim?

(A) Smoking rates have declined over the past decade.

(B) Non-smokers have a lower rate of lung disease than smokers.

(C) Lung disease can be influenced by other factors.

(D) Many smokers want to quit but find it challenging.

18. A recent survey indicates that using renewable energy sources reduces utility costs.

Which of the following would best support this finding?

(A) Renewable energy sources are increasingly available.

(B) Utility costs dropped by 15% in communities using solar and wind energy.

(C) Utility costs vary based on energy source.

(D) Renewable energy requires an initial investment.

19. An environmental study claims that planting trees reduces local temperatures.

Which piece of evidence best supports this claim?

(A) Trees provide shade in residential areas.

(B) Regions with dense tree cover have recorded lower average temperatures.

(C) Tree roots help prevent soil erosion.

(D) Trees require regular maintenance.

20. A sociologist argues that early education programs benefit children's cognitive development.

Which of the following findings would best support this argument?

(A) Children in early education programs perform better on cognitive tests.

(B) Many children enjoy early education activities.

(C) Early education programs can be costly.

(D) Cognitive development varies by age.

21. A financial report suggests that young adults save less for retirement compared to previous generations.

Which evidence would best support this suggestion?

(A) Retirement savings have declined among young adults.

(B) Young adults are taking on more debt than ever before.

(C) Many young adults delay homeownership.

(D) Retirement ages have gradually increased.

22. A healthcare study claims that people who sleep 7-8 hours per night have a lower risk of cardiovascular disease.

Which evidence would best support this study's claim?

(A) Sleep quality impacts overall health.

(B) Cardiovascular disease is more common in those who sleep less than 7 hours.

(C) People with cardiovascular disease often experience insomnia.

(D) Most people believe sleep is essential for health.

23. A report claims that electric cars help decrease air pollution.

Which of the following would best support this report?

(A) Electric cars are increasingly affordable.

(B) Studies show lower emissions in cities with more electric cars.

(C) More drivers are switching to electric vehicles.

(D) Electric cars do not require gasoline.

24. A historian suggests that cultural exchange during the Renaissance influenced European art.

Which evidence would best support this suggestion?

(A) Renaissance art techniques spread across Europe.

(B) Art styles remained isolated within regions.

(C) Artists focused on religious themes.

(D) Renaissance art was restricted to Italy.

25. A teacher argues that peer tutoring improves student performance in challenging subjects.

Which of the following would best support this argument?

(A) Students who participate in peer tutoring programs show higher grades in difficult subjects.

(B) Peer tutoring fosters social skills among students.

(C) Students often prefer studying alone.

(D) Challenging subjects require extra homework.

26. An environmental scientist states that recycling reduces landfill waste.

Which evidence would best support this claim?

(A) Recycling is a common practice in many countries.

(B) Studies show that recycling reduces landfill waste by 25%.

(C) Landfills are often located in rural areas.

(D) Recycling is difficult to implement.

27. A report suggests that young people are more likely to support renewable energy initiatives.

Which evidence would best support this suggestion?

(A) Surveys indicate 70% of young adults favor renewable energy.

(B) Older generations are less vocal about energy concerns.

(C) Many young people are aware of environmental issues.

(D) Support for renewable energy is increasing overall.

28. A psychologist proposes that spending time in nature improves mental health.

Which evidence would best support this proposal?

(A) People report feeling happier after spending time outdoors.

(B) Nature-based therapy is gaining popularity.

(C) Exercise improves mental health.

(D) Many people enjoy nature.

29. A nutrition expert argues that reducing sugar intake lowers the risk of type 2 diabetes.

Which of the following would best support this argument?

(A) People who consume less sugar have a lower incidence of type 2 diabetes.

(B) Sugar intake is linked to weight gain.

(C) Diabetes risk is higher in older adults.

(D) Many people eat sugar in moderation.

30. A sociologist claims that remote work can improve work-life balance for employees.

Which of the following pieces of evidence best supports this claim?

(A) Employees who work remotely report having more time with family.

(B) Remote work can reduce commuting costs.

(C) Many companies now offer hybrid work options.

(D) Remote workers often work longer hours.

Answer Explanations

1. (A) Emission records indicate a 40% decrease in pollutants over ten years – The journalist's claim about decreased pollution levels is directly supported by a documented reduction in emissions.

2. (A) Women often led key parts of the abolitionist movement – This choice highlights a historical role for women in social reform, aligning with the claim about their consistent involvement.

3. (C) Local businesses in small towns report revenue growth due to remote workers – Evidence of economic benefits for small-town businesses supports the economist's claim about remote work's positive impact on these areas.

4. (A) Teenagers report feeling less satisfied with their lives after using social media – This directly supports the psychologist's suggestion that social media may negatively impact teenage self-esteem.

5. (B) Studies show a 30% reduction in emissions from hybrid vehicles – The claim that hybrid cars reduce greenhouse gas emissions is directly supported by quantitative evidence.

6. (B) Studies show a 40% reduction in chronic illness among regular exercisers – This option provides quantitative data that directly supports the claim that regular exercise reduces the risk of chronic illnesses, making it the best answer.

7. (A) Forests help in water purification and maintaining watersheds – This choice supports the claim that deforestation affects clean water by showing forests' role in water supply, making (A) the best answer.

8. (B) Many urban residents report high stress levels – This option offers evidence that links urban living with higher stress, which supports the claim about mental health issues due to urbanization.

9. (B) Native plants attract local wildlife, which supports ecosystem health – The introduction of native plants attracting wildlife that benefits ecosystems directly supports the claim about biodiversity, making (B) correct.

10. (B) Statistics show that small businesses created 60% of new jobs in recent years – This option gives quantitative support to the claim that small businesses drive local job creation, aligning with the economist's statement.

11. (A) Certain crops have become more difficult to grow in warm climates – This choice provides evidence that rising temperatures can harm agricultural yield, which directly supports the claim about global warming's effects on agriculture.

12. (B) Students report feeling more involved in classes with hands-on projects – The positive response from students directly supports the idea that project-based learning improves engagement.

13. (B) Research shows that high-fiber diets are linked to a 30% lower risk of heart disease – This answer directly supports the nutritionist's claim with data on the link between fiber intake and reduced heart disease risk.

14. (C) Populations of endangered species have increased in protected areas – This choice directly supports the claim by providing evidence that conservation areas help endangered species thrive.

15. (A) People who read frequently have larger vocabularies than non-readers – The relationship between frequent reading and vocabulary size directly supports the claim about vocabulary improvement through reading.

16. (B) Companies with high employee satisfaction see a 20% boost in productivity – This option provides data that directly supports the claim that employee satisfaction correlates with increased productivity.

17. (B) Non-smokers have a lower rate of lung disease than smokers – This evidence directly supports the doctor's claim that quitting smoking can reduce lung disease risk.

18. (B) Utility costs dropped by 15% in communities using solar and wind energy – This option provides quantitative evidence supporting the claim that renewable energy reduces utility costs.

19. (B) Regions with dense tree cover have recorded lower average temperatures – This choice provides direct evidence that planting trees can reduce local temperatures, supporting the claim.

20. (A) Children in early education programs perform better on cognitive tests – This option provides direct evidence of the cognitive benefits of early education, supporting the sociologist's claim.

21. (A) Retirement savings have declined among young adults – The decline in savings directly supports the financial report's claim that young adults save less for retirement.

22. (B) Cardiovascular disease is more common in those who sleep less than 7 hours – This option directly supports the claim that getting enough sleep reduces cardiovascular disease risk.

23. (B) Studies show lower emissions in cities with more electric cars – This choice provides direct evidence that electric cars help reduce air pollution, supporting the report's claim.

24. (A) Renaissance art techniques spread across Europe – This option supports the idea that cultural exchange during the Renaissance influenced art styles across Europe.

25. (A) Students who participate in peer tutoring programs show higher grades in difficult subjects – The improvement in grades among students in peer tutoring programs directly supports the teacher's argument.

26. (B) Studies show that recycling reduces landfill waste by 25% – This quantitative data directly supports the scientist's claim that recycling reduces landfill waste.

27. (A) Surveys indicate 70% of young adults favor renewable energy – This survey result directly supports the report's claim about young people's support for renewable energy.

28. (A) People report feeling happier after spending time outdoors – This feedback directly supports the psychologist's proposal that nature improves mental health.

29. (A) People who consume less sugar have a lower incidence of type 2 diabetes – This option directly supports the argument by providing evidence linking low sugar intake with reduced diabetes risk.

30. (A) Employees who work remotely report having more time with family – The increased family time reported by remote employees directly supports the claim that remote work improves work-life balance.

Inferences

In the SAT Reading and Writing section, "Inferences" questions test your ability to read between the lines, drawing logical conclusions based on the information presented in a passage. Inference skills require you to go beyond what is explicitly stated, using context clues and supporting details to arrive at an implied meaning or understanding. These questions often hinge on subtle hints within the text, so it's important to consider not only what is said but also what is suggested.

Strategies for answering inference questions include:

- **Identifying Contextual Clues**: Pay attention to keywords, tone, and surrounding details that give insight into the author's intended message.
- **Understanding Implicit Relationships:** Look for underlying connections between ideas, even if they aren't directly stated.

- Avoiding Over-Interpretation: Choose inferences that are directly supported by the text, rather than making assumptions not grounded in the passage.

Mastering inference skills helps you understand deeper meanings and gain insights that enhance overall comprehension. Let's dive into practice questions to refine this essential skill!

Questions

1. A scientist notes that certain fish species are thriving in waters with higher oxygen levels.

Based on this observation, what can we infer about these fish species?

(A) They rely on low-oxygen environments.

(B) They are likely adapted to higher oxygen levels.

(C) They prefer shallow waters.

(D) They are unaffected by oxygen levels.

2. A manager observes that team members perform better when they receive constructive feedback regularly.

What is a reasonable inference based on this observation?

(A) Team members dislike feedback.

(B) Constructive feedback boosts performance.

(C) Feedback negatively impacts team morale.

(D) Team members prefer to work independently.

3. A nutritionist finds that people who consume a high-fiber diet have fewer digestive issues.

What can we infer about fiber from this observation?

(A) Fiber may aid digestion.

(B) Fiber increases digestive issues.

(C) Fiber causes nutrient loss.

(D) People on a high-fiber diet have poor digestion.

4. An economist points out that spending in local businesses increased after a new mall opened.

What is the most likely inference based on this observation?

(A) The mall has had no effect on local spending.

(B) The new mall attracted more shoppers to the area.

(C) Spending decreased in nearby cities.

(D) Local businesses are unaffected by the new mall.

5. A recent study shows that students who sleep 8 hours before an exam perform better than those who sleep less.

What can we infer from this study?

(A) Sleep has no effect on exam performance.

(B) Sleep may improve cognitive function in students.

(C) Students perform better without sleep.

(D) Only 8 hours of sleep is beneficial.

6. A teacher notices that students who participate in group discussions tend to perform better on assessments.

What is a reasonable inference based on this observation?

(A) Group discussions do not benefit students.

(B) Participation in discussions enhances student learning.

(C) Group discussions increase students' stress.

(D) Students perform best when they study alone.

7. A researcher observes that when city parks are well-maintained, more people visit them.

What can we infer from this observation?

(A) People avoid well-maintained parks.

(B) Maintenance levels impact park visitation.

(C) Most people do not use parks regularly.

(D) Park maintenance has no effect on attendance.

8. A chef notices that dishes with fresh ingredients are more popular among customers.

What inference can we draw from this observation?

(A) Fresh ingredients make dishes more appealing to customers.

(B) Customers prefer frozen ingredients.

(C) Customers do not care about ingredient quality.

(D) Fresh ingredients lower food quality.

9. A sports coach finds that athletes who train consistently perform better in competitions.

What can be inferred from this finding?

(A) Consistent training improves athletic performance.

(B) Training reduces athletes' performance levels.

(C) Athletes prefer to avoid training.

(D) Training has no effect on performance.

10. An environmental scientist notes that air quality improves in regions with more trees.

What is a reasonable inference from this observation?

(A) Trees have no effect on air quality.

(B) Trees may play a role in improving air quality.

(C) Air quality is worse in forested regions.

(D) Trees make air quality worse.

11. A librarian observes that patrons who receive book recommendations are more likely to borrow books.

What can be inferred from this observation?

(A) Recommendations discourage patrons from borrowing books.

(B) Book recommendations can encourage borrowing.

(C) Patrons prefer selecting books independently.

(D) Most patrons ignore recommendations.

12. A company finds that employees who receive ongoing training are more productive.

What is a reasonable inference?

(A) Ongoing training increases productivity.

(B) Training has no effect on productivity.

(C) Employees are less productive with training.

(D) Employees prefer to work without training.

13. A health study reveals that people who drink water before meals consume fewer calories.

What can we infer from this finding?

(A) Drinking water increases calorie intake.

(B) Drinking water may reduce calorie intake.

(C) Drinking water has no impact on appetite.

(D) People avoid drinking water before meals.

14. A tour guide notices that visitors enjoy historical tours more when there are interactive exhibits.

What can we infer?

(A) Interactive exhibits enhance visitors' tour experiences.

(B) Visitors dislike interactive exhibits.

(C) Interactive exhibits do not affect visitor enjoyment.

(D) Historical tours are less popular than other tours.

15. A fitness trainer observes that clients who set specific fitness goals are more motivated.

What is a reasonable inference?

(A) Goal-setting may increase motivation.

(B) Specific goals decrease motivation.

(C) Motivation is unrelated to fitness goals.

(D) Clients prefer to avoid setting fitness goals.

16. A principal notes that students who participate in extracurricular activities have higher GPAs.

What can be inferred from this observation?

(A) Extracurriculars may correlate with higher academic performance.

(B) Extracurriculars decrease GPA.

(C) Students avoid extracurricular activities.

(D) Participation has no effect on GPA.

17. A study shows that residents of coastal areas are more concerned about climate change.

What is a reasonable inference?

(A) Proximity to the coast increases climate change awareness.

(B) Coastal residents are indifferent to climate change.

(C) People far from coasts are more concerned.

(D) Climate change only affects coastal areas.

18. A recent report shows that people who read daily have improved concentration skills."

What can be inferred from this finding?

(A) Daily reading may enhance concentration.

(B) Reading reduces concentration skills.

(C) Concentration is unrelated to reading habits.

(D) People prefer not to read daily.

19. A college professor notices that students who attend office hours are more confident about exams.

What is a reasonable inference?

(A) Office hours do not benefit students.

(B) Attending office hours may boost confidence.

(C) Students avoid attending office hours.

(D) Office hours increase students' stress.

20. A car manufacturer finds that hybrid car owners report higher satisfaction with fuel efficiency.

What can we infer from this observation?

(A) Hybrid cars may provide better fuel efficiency.

(B) Fuel efficiency is unrelated to car satisfaction.

(C) Hybrid owners are unhappy with fuel efficiency.

(D) Hybrid cars are not fuel-efficient.

21. A wildlife biologist observes that deer populations are more abundant in protected forests.

What is a reasonable inference?

(A) Protected forests may help support deer populations.

(B) Deer avoid protected areas.

(C) Deer populations thrive in urban areas.

(D) Protected forests decrease deer numbers.

22. A sales manager notices that customers who try products before purchasing are more likely to buy them.

What can be inferred from this observation?

(A) Product trials may increase purchase likelihood.

(B) Customers avoid trying products.

(C) Trying products decreases sales.

(D) Trials make customers less interested in buying.

23. A poll shows that people who work from home are more likely to report a better work-life balance.

What can we infer from this poll?

(A) Working from home may improve work-life balance.

(B) People dislike working from home.

(C) Work-life balance is unaffected by work location.

(D) Work-life balance decreases with remote work.

24. A dietitian finds that people who eat breakfast daily have more energy throughout the day.

What is a reasonable inference?

(A) Breakfast may boost daily energy levels.

(B) Breakfast decreases energy levels.

(C) Energy levels are unrelated to breakfast.

(D) People avoid eating breakfast.

25. A social worker observes that individuals involved in community service report higher life satisfaction.

What can we infer from this observation?

(A) Community service may enhance life satisfaction.

(B) Life satisfaction decreases with community involvement.

(C) Community service has no effect on happiness.

(D) Most people avoid community service.

26. A company finds that employees who take regular breaks are less likely to experience burnout.

What is a reasonable inference?

(A) Taking breaks may reduce burnout risk.

(B) Breaks increase burnout.

(C) Burnout is unrelated to taking breaks.

(D) Employees prefer working without breaks.

27. A scientist notes that plants exposed to sunlight grow taller than those kept in the shade.

What can we infer from this observation?

(A) Sunlight may encourage plant growth.

(B) Shade improves plant growth.

(C) Sunlight has no effect on plants.

(D) Plants prefer growing in the dark.

28. A teacher observes that students who take notes during lectures remember more information.

What is a reasonable inference?

(A) Note-taking may improve memory retention.

(B) Students remember more without notes.

(C) Note-taking has no effect on memory.

(D) Students avoid taking notes.

29. A transportation study finds that people who commute by bike have higher physical fitness levels.

What can we infer from this finding?

(A) Biking may contribute to better fitness.

(B) Commuting by bike reduces fitness.

(C) Fitness is unaffected by biking.

(D) People avoid biking.

30. A survey reveals that shoppers who plan purchases in advance spend less than those who don't.

What is a reasonable inference from this survey?

(A) Planned purchases may help reduce spending.

(B) Planning purchases increases spending.

(C) Spending is unrelated to shopping plans.

(D) Shoppers dislike planning purchases.

Answer Explanations

1. (B) They are likely adapted to higher oxygen levels – Since these fish thrive in high-oxygen waters, we can infer that they have adaptations suited for these conditions.

2. (B) Constructive feedback boosts performance – Regular constructive feedback positively impacts team members' performance, making (B) the best inference.

3. (A) Fiber may aid digestion – The nutritionist's observation about fewer digestive issues among high-fiber consumers suggests a positive link between fiber and digestion.

4. (B) The new mall attracted more shoppers to the area – Increased spending in local businesses after the mall's opening suggests that the mall draws additional customers to the area.

5. (B) Sleep may improve cognitive function in students – Better exam performance after 8 hours of sleep suggests that sufficient sleep could enhance cognitive performance.

6. (B) Participation in discussions enhances student learning – Students who discuss in groups perform better, suggesting that discussions positively impact learning.

7. (B) Maintenance levels impact park visitation – The increase in visitors to well-maintained parks suggests a link between park maintenance and attendance.

8. (A) Fresh ingredients make dishes more appealing to customers – The chef's observation suggests that fresh ingredients improve customer satisfaction.

9. (A) Consistent training improves athletic performance – The coach's observation that regular training leads to better performance suggests a positive impact of training on athletes.

10. (B) Trees may play a role in improving air quality – The scientist's observation of improved air quality in areas with more trees implies that trees positively affect air quality.

11. (B) Book recommendations can encourage borrowing – The librarian's observation suggests that patrons are more likely to borrow books when given recommendations, indicating that recommendations boost borrowing.

12. (A) Ongoing training increases productivity – The company's findings suggest a link between regular training and higher productivity, making (A) the best inference.

13. (B) Drinking water may reduce calorie intake – The health study's observation that people consume fewer calories after drinking water implies a connection between water intake and reduced calorie consumption.

14. (A) Interactive exhibits enhance visitors' tour experiences – The tour guide's observation suggests that interactive exhibits improve visitor enjoyment.

15. (A) Goal-setting may increase motivation – The trainer's observation implies that setting specific fitness goals could boost motivation in clients.

16. (A) Extracurriculars may correlate with higher academic performance – The principal's note suggests a link between extracurricular participation and better academic outcomes.

17. (A) Proximity to the coast increases climate change awareness – The observation suggests that living near the coast may heighten awareness of climate change issues.

18. (A) Daily reading may enhance concentration – The report suggests a connection between daily reading habits and improved concentration skills.

19. (B) Attending office hours may boost confidence – The professor's observation implies that students feel more confident about exams after attending office hours.

20. (A) Hybrid cars may provide better fuel efficiency – The car manufacturer's observation implies that hybrid cars offer better fuel efficiency, which enhances owner satisfaction.

21. (A) Protected forests may help support deer populations – The biologist's observation suggests that protected areas support higher deer populations, making (A) the best inference.

22. (A) Product trials may increase purchase likelihood – The manager's note suggests that allowing customers to try products boosts their chances of making a purchase.

23. (A) Working from home may improve work-life balance – The poll suggests a positive impact of remote work on employees' work-life balance.

24. (A) Breakfast may boost daily energy levels – The dietitian's observation suggests a positive link between eating breakfast and having more energy.

25. (A) Community service may enhance life satisfaction – The social worker's observation suggests that involvement in community service correlates with higher life satisfaction.

26. (A) Taking breaks may reduce burnout risk – The company's findings imply that regular breaks reduce the likelihood of burnout.

27. (A) Sunlight may encourage plant growth – The scientist's observation suggests that sunlight positively affects plant growth.

28. (A) Note-taking may improve memory retention – The teacher's observation implies that students who take notes are better at remembering information.

29. (A) Biking may contribute to better fitness – The study's findings suggest that commuting by bike could improve physical fitness levels.

30. (A) Planned purchases may help reduce spending – The survey's results imply that planning purchases could help shoppers control their spending.

CHAPTER 3

Writing Practice Questions

Number and Tense Agreement

In the SAT Writing and Language section, "Number and Tense Agreement" questions test your ability to match subjects with verbs in both number (singular or plural) and tense (past, present, or future) consistently within a sentence or passage. Ensuring correct number and tense agreement is key for clear and grammatically correct writing, as it helps readers easily follow the time frame and subject focus of each statement.

Key strategies for these questions include:

- **Identifying the Subject**: Determine whether the subject is singular or plural to match it correctly with the verb.
- **Consistent Tense Usage**: Ensure that the tense remains logical and consistent within the sentence or paragraph, unless there's a clear reason to shift (like indicating a change in time).
- **Noting Collective Nouns**: Nouns like "team," "jury," and "committee" are singular when acting as a single unit but may take plural verbs if emphasizing individual members.

Mastering these skills will improve both grammar and clarity, ensuring that each sentence is accurate and well-structured. Now, let's dive into practice questions to refine this important skill!

Questions

1. The committee _____ their final decision tomorrow.

(A) announce

(B) will announce

(C) are announcing

(D) has announced

2. Each of the students _____ responsible for completing the project by the deadline.

(A) were

(B) are

(C) is

(D) have been

3. The team, along with the coach, _____ scheduled to arrive at noon.

(A) were

(B) was

(C) are

(D) have been

4. Neither of the twins _____ interested in attending the party.

(A) were

(B) is

(C) are

(D) has

5. The data from the experiments _____ conclusive.

(A) is

(B) are

(C) was

(D) has been

6. Every one of the books on the shelves _____ been read by her.

(A) have

(B) has

(C) had

(D) are

7. The collection of rare coins _____ sold to a private collector last year.

(A) were

(B) are

(C) was

(D) have been

8. One of the players _____ injured during the game.

(A) were

(B) is

(C) have been

(D) was

9. Either the manager or the employees _____ responsible for submitting the report.

(A) is

(B) are

(C) were

(D) being

10. The scissors _____ on the desk.

(A) is

(B) were

(C) has

(D) was

11. The jury _____ reached a unanimous verdict.

(A) have

(B) has

(C) is

(D) are

12. Several students _____ planning to study abroad next semester.

(A) is

(B) was

(C) has

(D) are

13. A group of scientists _____ investigating the effects of climate change.

(A) are

(B) have

(C) is

(D) has

14. The book, along with its sequels, _____ popular among young readers.

(A) are

(B) was

(C) were

(D) have been

15. The members of the committee _____ scheduled a meeting for next week.

(A) has

(B) have

(C) is

(D) was

16. The committee members _____ presenting their findings next week.

(A) is

(B) was

(C) are

(D) has

17. One of the greatest challenges _____ keeping up with changing technology.

(A) is

(B) are

(C) were

(D) have been

18. Each of the athletes _____ hoping to win the competition.

(A) are

(B) were

(C) was

(D) is

19. The number of applicants _____ steadily increasing each year.

(A) are

(B) have

(C) was

(D) is

20. None of the students _____ aware of the new policy.

(A) were

(B) was

(C) are

(D) have

21. The manager, as well as the team members, _____ attending the conference.

(A) is

(B) were

(C) are

(D) has

22. A collection of essays _____ on the shelf.

(A) were

(B) is

(C) has

(D) have

23. The team _____ planning their annual retreat.

(A) were

(B) has

(C) is

(D) are

24. Both of the candidates _____ well-prepared for the interview.

(A) was

(B) were

(C) is

(D) has

25. The board of directors _____ agreed to the new terms.

(A) have

(B) is

(C) was

(D) has

26. One of the documents _____ missing from the file.

(A) were

(B) was

(C) are

(D) have

27. The variety of plants _____ diverse in this region.

(A) was

(B) were

(C) is

(D) are

28. The committee _____ divided on the issue.

(A) is

(B) are

(C) has

(D) were

29. The team members, along with their coach, _____ ready for the match.

(A) is

(B) are

(C) was

(D) have

30. Everyone in the group _____ responsible for their assigned tasks.

(A) were

(B) was

(C) are

(D) is

Answer Explanations

1. (B) will announce – "Committee" is a collective noun, treated as singular here, so the singular future tense "will announce" is correct.

2. (C) is – "Each" is singular, so "is" correctly matches in number and tense.

3. (B) was – "Team" is singular, and "along with the coach" does not change the number, making "was" correct.

4. (B) is – "Neither" is singular, so "is" matches the singular requirement.

5. (A) is – "Data" is treated as a singular collective noun here, making "is" the correct form.

6. (B) has – "Every one" is singular, so "has" aligns with the singular subject.

7. (C) was – "Collection" is singular, meaning "was" is appropriate.

8. (D) was – "One of the players" is singular, so "was" is the correct form.

9. (A) is – When using "either/or," the verb agrees with the nearest subject. Here, "manager" is singular, so "is" is correct.

10. (B) were – "Scissors" is always treated as plural, so "were" is appropriate.

11. (B) has – "Jury" is treated as a collective singular noun here, so "has" is the correct form.

12. (D) are – "Several" is plural, so "are" is the appropriate form.

13. (C) is – "Group" is treated as singular, so "is" is the correct choice.

14. (B) was – "Book" is singular, and "along with its sequels" does not change the singular form, making "was" correct.

15. (B) have – "Members" is plural, so "have" is appropriate here.

16. (C) are – "Members" is plural, so "are" matches the subject in number and tense.

17. (A) is – "One" is the subject, and it is singular, so "is" is the correct choice.

18. (D) is – "Each" is singular, so "is" is appropriate to match the subject.

19. (D) is – "The number" is treated as singular, requiring the singular verb "is."

20. (A) were – "None" can be singular or plural; here, it matches "students" in a plural sense, so "were" is correct.

21. (A) is – "The manager" is the main subject, and it's singular, making "is" the best choice.

22. (B) is – "Collection" is a singular noun, so "is" is appropriate.

23. (C) is – "Team" is treated as singular here, so "is" is the correct verb form.

24. (B) were – "Both" is plural, so "were" correctly matches the plural subject.

25. (A) have – "Board of directors" is a collective noun that can be treated as plural here, so "have" is appropriate.

26. (B) was – "One" is singular, so "was" is the correct verb form.

27. (C) is – "Variety" is singular, so "is" is appropriate for this sentence.

28. (A) is – "Committee" is treated as a singular noun here, so "is" correctly matches it.

29. (B) are – "Team members" is plural, so "are" is appropriate.

30. (D) is – "Everyone" is singular, so "is" is the correct verb form.

Punctuation

In the SAT Writing and Language section, "Punctuation" questions assess your understanding of how to use punctuation marks like commas, colons, semicolons, and dashes effectively to enhance clarity and meaning. Proper punctuation not only ensures grammatical accuracy but also helps guide readers smoothly through ideas and relationships within sentences.

Key strategies for mastering punctuation questions include:

- **Identifying Clause Types**: Recognize whether you're working with independent or dependent clauses, as this will guide the correct punctuation, like commas for dependent clauses and semicolons or periods for independent ones.
- **Introducing Lists or Explanations**: Use colons to introduce lists, examples, or elaborations and ensure clarity in complex sentences.
- **Creating Emphasis or Contrast**: Dashes are useful for setting off important information or creating contrast, while commas help clarify series or pause phrases naturally.

By understanding punctuation's role in sentence structure, you can enhance sentence flow, ensure grammatical precision, and avoid common errors. Let's begin with practice questions to reinforce these punctuation skills!

Questions

1. The professor introduced the topic of cognitive biases: _____ different ways people perceive and process information.

Which punctuation completes the sentence?

(A) showing how

(B) to illustrate the

(C) it is

(D) including

2. Her report was thorough and insightful _____ she highlighted key findings and offered recommendations.

Which punctuation best completes the sentence?

(A) ,

(B) ;

(C) :

(D) –

3. The museum's new exhibit includes pieces by famous artists: Van Gogh, Monet, and Picasso.

Which punctuation best completes the sentence?

(A) ,

(B) :

(C) ;

(D) .

4. Her friends were all busy with their own schedules _____ she decided to go to the concert alone.

Which punctuation completes the sentence?

(A) ;

(B) ,

(C) :

(D) –

5. The CEO's speech was impactful, emphasizing three main goals: innovation, efficiency, and sustainability.

Which punctuation best completes the sentence?

(A) ,

(B) ;

(C) :

(D) –

6. After months of planning _____ the team finally launched their new project.

Which punctuation best completes the sentence?

(A) ,

(B) ;

(C) :

(D) –

7. The ingredients for the recipe are simple _____ flour, sugar, and eggs.

Which punctuation completes the sentence?

(A) ,

(B) ;

(C) :

(D) –

8. To be eligible, you must meet these requirements _____ be 18 or older, have a valid ID, and pass the background check.

Which punctuation completes the sentence?

(A) ;

(B) ,

(C) :

(D) –

9. Her favorite subjects include history, math, and _____ science.

Which punctuation best completes the sentence?

(A) ,

(B) :

(C) ;

(D) –

10. I enjoy traveling _____ however, I find it exhausting sometimes.

Which punctuation completes the sentence?

(A) ,

(B) ;

(C) :

(D) –

11. The project required three things _____ dedication, teamwork, and persistence.

Which punctuation best completes the sentence?

(A) ,

(B) ;

(C) :

(D) –

12. He is an accomplished musician _____ he plays both the guitar and the piano exceptionally well.

Which punctuation completes the sentence?

(A) ,

(B) ;

(C) :

(D) –

13. The author's message was clear _____ believe in yourself, work hard, and be patient.

Which punctuation completes the sentence?

(A) ,

(B) ;

(C) :

(D) –

14. The company focuses on three core values _____ integrity, quality, and customer satisfaction.

Which punctuation best completes the sentence?

(A) ,

(B) ;

(C) :

(D) –

15. Their meeting covered various topics _____ marketing strategies, budget plans, and upcoming projects.

Which punctuation completes the sentence?

(A) ,

(B) ;

(C) :

(D) –

16. We visited several landmarks in Rome _____ the Colosseum, the Pantheon, and the Roman Forum.

Which punctuation completes the sentence?

(A) ,

(B) ;

(C) :

(D) –

17. She was determined to succeed _____ despite the challenges she faced.

Which punctuation best completes the sentence?

(A) ,

(B) ;

(C) :

(D) –

18. The students studied three subjects: math, _____ science, and literature.

Which punctuation best completes the sentence?

(A) ,

(B) ;

(C) :

(D) –

19. He kept a close eye on the stock market _____ hoping to capitalize on any shifts.

Which punctuation completes the sentence?

(A) ,

(B) ;

(C) :

(D) –

20. She was happy to help _____ however, she had limited time to spare.

Which punctuation completes the sentence?

(A) ,

(B) ;

(C) :

(D) –

21. The proposal outlined three phases _____ research, development, and implementation.

Which punctuation best completes the sentence?

(A) ,

(B) ;

(C) :

(D) –

22. He bought the following groceries: milk, bread, and eggs.

Which punctuation best completes the sentence?

(A) ,

(B) ;

(C) :

(D) –

23. Her goals are ambitious _____ she plans to start her own business, earn a degree, and travel abroad.

Which punctuation completes the sentence?

(A) ,

(B) ;

(C) :

(D) –

24. They explored different career paths _____ including medicine, law, and engineering.

Which punctuation best completes the sentence?

(A) ,

(B) ;

(C) :

(D) –

25. The writer's style was unique _____ it blended humor with profound insight.

Which punctuation completes the sentence?

(A) ,

(B) ;

(C) :

(D) –

26. My favorite colors are blue, green, and _____ purple.

Which punctuation best completes the sentence?

(A) ,

(B) ;

(C) :

(D) –

27. The doctor suggested several lifestyle changes _____ diet, exercise, and sleep.

Which punctuation completes the sentence?

(A) ,

(B) ;

(C) :

(D) –

28. The team succeeded _____ despite the odds being against them.

Which punctuation completes the sentence?

(A) ,

(B) ;

(C) :

(D) –

29. The presentation included three parts _____ an introduction, a detailed analysis, and a conclusion.

Which punctuation completes the sentence?

(A) ,

(B) ;

(C) :

(D) –

30. He is skilled in two areas _____ software development and project management.

Which punctuation completes the sentence?

(A) ,

(B) ;

(C) :

(D) –

31. His plan was simple _____ save more, spend less, and invest wisely.

Which punctuation best completes the sentence?

(A) ,

(B) ;

(C) :

(D) –

32. The novel's themes include friendship, courage, and _____ loyalty.

Which punctuation best completes the sentence?

(A) ,

(B) ;

(C) :

(D) –

33. We have two goals _____ to increase revenue and to improve customer satisfaction.

Which punctuation best completes the sentence?

(A) ,

(B) ;

(C) :

(D) –

34. He wanted to visit several countries _____ France, Italy, and Spain.

Which punctuation best completes the sentence?

(A) ,

(B) ;

(C) :

(D) –

35. The lecture covered three topics _____ biology, chemistry, and physics.

Which punctuation best completes the sentence?

(A) ,

(B) ;

(C) :

(D) –

36. Their project was ambitious _____ however, they had a well-organized plan.

Which punctuation best completes the sentence?

(A) ,

(B) ;

(C) :

(D) –

37. The bookstore offers a variety of genres: mystery, science fiction, and romance.

Which punctuation best completes the sentence?

(A) ,

(B) :

(C) ;

(D) –

38. She was excited to try new activities _____ skiing, hiking, and sailing.

Which punctuation best completes the sentence?

(A) ,

(B) ;

(C) :

(D) –

39. The professor emphasized three skills _____ critical thinking, analysis, and communication.

Which punctuation best completes the sentence?

(A) ,

(B) ;

(C) :

(D) –

40. Their efforts were successful _____ consequently, the project received funding.

Which punctuation best completes the sentence?

(A) ,

(B) ;

(C) :

(D) –

41. The company announced its priorities: customer service, product quality, and sustainability.

Which punctuation best completes the sentence?

(A) ,

(B) :

(C) ;

(D) –

42. He excelled in three sports _____ basketball, soccer, and tennis.

Which punctuation best completes the sentence?

(A) ,

(B) ;

(C) :

(D) –

43. The workshop covered several skills _____ time management, communication, and leadership.

Which punctuation best completes the sentence?

(A) ,

(B) ;

(C) :

(D) –

44. They met to discuss several important topics _____ budget, timeline, and project scope.

Which punctuation best completes the sentence?

(A) ,

(B) ;

(C) :

(D) –

45. The painting depicted several colors _____ blue, green, and yellow.

Which punctuation best completes the sentence?

(A) ,

(B) ;

(C) :

(D) –

46. He had three main hobbies: reading, cooking, and gardening.

Which punctuation best completes the sentence?

(A) ,

(B) :

(C) ;

(D) –

47. The report included key metrics _____ revenue growth, market share, and customer retention.

Which punctuation best completes the sentence?

(A) ,

(B) ;

(C) :

(D) –

48. She wore her favorite colors _____ red, black, and white.

Which punctuation best completes the sentence?

(A) ,

(B) ;

(C) :

(D) –

49. The writer's inspiration came from three places _____ nature, art, and music.

Which punctuation best completes the sentence?

(A) ,

(B) ;

(C) :

(D) –

50. The program's goals were ambitious _____ however, the team was motivated to achieve them.

Which punctuation best completes the sentence?

(A) ,

(B) ;

(C) :

(D) –

Answer Explanations

1. (D) including – A colon introduces specific examples or clarifications, making it appropriate here.

2. (B) ; – A semicolon effectively connects two related independent clauses.

3. (B) : – A colon introduces a list of items, so it is correct here.

4. (A) ; – A semicolon joins two independent but related clauses, suitable here.

5. (C) : – The colon introduces a list of goals, aligning with standard punctuation rules.

6. (A) , – A comma sets off an introductory clause.

7. (C) : – The colon introduces examples, making it the correct punctuation.

8. (C) : – The colon introduces the list of requirements.

9. (A) , – A comma is appropriate for listing.

10. (B) ; – A semicolon connects two related independent clauses.

11. (C) : – The colon introduces a list.

12. (B) ; – A semicolon correctly connects related ideas in independent clauses.

13. (C) : – The colon introduces a list of the author's message.

14. (C) : – The colon introduces the company's core values.

15. (C) : – The colon introduces the list of topics covered.

16. (C) : – The colon introduces the landmarks in Rome.

17. (D) – – The dash introduces a contrasting clause.

18. (A) , – A comma correctly separates list items.

19. (A) , – A comma separates the clause for smoother reading.

20. (B) ; – A semicolon connects related independent clauses.

21. (C) : – The colon introduces a list.

22. (C) : – The colon introduces a list of groceries.

23. (B) ; – The semicolon effectively connects independent but related ideas.

24. (C) : – A colon introduces the examples that follow.

25. (B) ; – A semicolon appropriately links the two related ideas as independent clauses.

26. (A) , – A comma is suitable for this list, keeping the series consistent.

27. (C) : – A colon effectively introduces the list of changes suggested by the doctor.

28. (D) – – The dash introduces a clause that contrasts with the team's success.

29. (C) : – The colon introduces the parts of the presentation.

30. (C) : – A colon introduces the areas in which he is skilled.

31. (C) : – The colon introduces the list of goals that follows.

32. (A) , – A comma is appropriate here to separate items in a list.

33. (C) : – A colon introduces the specific goals.

34. (C) : – The colon introduces the list of countries he wants to visit.

35. (C) : – The colon introduces the list of lecture topics.

36. (B) ; – A semicolon connects two related independent clauses.

37. (B) : – The colon introduces the list of genres at the bookstore.

38. (C) : – The colon introduces the specific activities.

39. (C) : – A colon introduces the list of emphasized skills.

40. (B) ; – A semicolon appropriately connects two related clauses.

41. (B) : – The colon introduces the company's priorities.

42. (C) : – A colon introduces the list of sports.

43. (C) : – The colon introduces the specific skills covered in the workshop.

44. (C) : – The colon introduces a list of important topics discussed.

45. (C) : – The colon introduces the colors depicted in the painting.

46. (B) : – The colon introduces the hobbies that follow.

47. (C) : – The colon introduces the list of key metrics.

48. (C) : – The colon introduces the specific colors she wore.

49. (C) : – A colon introduces the writer's sources of inspiration.

50. (B) ; – The semicolon connects the two independent clauses.

Sentence Structure and Organization

In the SAT Writing and Language section, "Sentence Structure and Organization" questions assess your ability to arrange ideas within and between sentences logically and clearly. These questions require you to determine the best way to connect, sequence, or revise sentences to improve readability and coherence. This skill ensures that each sentence flows naturally and that each paragraph presents ideas in a meaningful and organized manner.

Key strategies for answering these questions include:

- **Recognizing Logical Transitions**: Look for transition words that signal relationships, such as cause-and-effect, contrast, or addition, and ensure they align with the sentence's intended meaning.
- **Ensuring Consistent Structure**: Maintain parallel structure when listing ideas or actions, as this enhances readability.
- **Organizing Ideas Clearly**: Evaluate whether the order of sentences makes the passage easy to follow. Be mindful of shifts in topics or ideas that could confuse readers and choose the organization that best develops the argument or explanation.

Mastering sentence structure and organization enhances clarity, making writing more engaging and effective. Let's dive into practice questions to strengthen these essential skills!

Questions

1. The report highlighted various strategies, focusing on data analysis and _____ effective communication.

Which choice best completes the sentence?

(A) involving

(B) involved in

(C) involves

(D) involve

2. Despite their success, the team members were humble _____ they knew there was more work to do.

Which choice best completes the sentence?

(A) since

(B) while

(C) and

(D) even though

3. The committee decided on a plan _____ will ensure long-term growth.

Which choice best completes the sentence?

(A) who

(B) which

(C) what

(D) where

4. Studying for exams requires dedication, patience, and _____ effective time management.

Which choice best completes the sentence?

(A) the implementation of

(B) being managed by

(C) manages

(D) managing

5. The project, _____ was initially expected to finish in six months, took nearly a year to complete.

Which choice best completes the sentence?

(A) that

(B) which

(C) where

(D) who

6. She has a talent for music _____ she practices the piano daily.

Which choice best completes the sentence?

(A) and

(B) while

(C) because

(D) although

7. Many students find online courses beneficial, _____ they offer flexibility and convenience.

Which choice best completes the sentence?

(A) therefore

(B) because

(C) but

(D) so

8. The manager, _____ made significant contributions to the project, was recognized by her peers.

Which choice best completes the sentence?

(A) that

(B) who

(C) whom

(D) which

9. He missed the event, _____ he was not informed about the change in schedule.

Which choice best completes the sentence?

(A) since

(B) but

(C) therefore

(D) although

10. The athlete trains rigorously _____ she wants to qualify for the Olympics.

Which choice best completes the sentence?

(A) if

(B) so

(C) because

(D) but

11. The concert, _____ was held outdoors, attracted a large audience.

Which choice best completes the sentence?

(A) which

(B) that

(C) whom

(D) where

12. Effective leaders inspire others _____ they can reach their full potential.

Which choice best completes the sentence?

(A) while

(B) so

(C) that

(D) as

13. Her achievements were remarkable, _____ she was recognized as a role model.

Which choice best completes the sentence?

(A) therefore

(B) however

(C) since

(D) but

14. The document was revised _____ it was accurate and up-to-date.

Which choice best completes the sentence?

(A) so

(B) if

(C) so that

(D) while

15. A sustainable approach requires planning, commitment, and _____ long-term vision.

Which choice best completes the sentence?

(A) to be

(B) a

(C) being

(D) having

16. In 2019, the museum welcomed over one million visitors, _____ the highest attendance on record.

Which choice best completes the sentence?

(A) so

(B) making

(C) thus

(D) therefore

17. The presentation was informative, _____ it could have been more engaging.

Which choice best completes the sentence?

(A) if

(B) although

(C) while

(D) so

18. Students are encouraged to participate in extracurricular activities, _____ they can develop new skills.

Which choice best completes the sentence?

(A) because

(B) therefore

(C) so

(D) while

19. She appreciated the feedback, _____ she felt it was constructive.

Which choice best completes the sentence?

(A) because

(B) as

(C) since

(D) although

20. The plan needs to be approved _____ it can be implemented.

Which choice best completes the sentence?

(A) before

(B) after

(C) because

(D) if

21. She completed the project ahead of schedule, _____ impressed her supervisor.

Which choice best completes the sentence?

(A) which

(B) who

(C) that

(D) it

22. To succeed in this role, one needs dedication, persistence, and _____ ability to adapt.

Which choice best completes the sentence?

(A) an

(B) a

(C) the

(D) none

23. The building was renovated to include a library, a cafe, and _____ outdoor seating area.

Which choice best completes the sentence?

(A) an

(B) a

(C) the

(D) those

24. She excelled in her studies, _____ her professors often praised her work ethic.

Which choice best completes the sentence?

(A) and

(B) so

(C) but

(D) for

25. The film received critical acclaim, _____ it was considered groundbreaking.

Which choice best completes the sentence?

(A) if

(B) for

(C) yet

(D) and

26. The policy changes aim to improve efficiency, productivity, and _____ employee satisfaction.

Which choice best completes the sentence?

(A) creating

(B) create

(C) created

(D) none

27. A team of researchers conducted the experiment _____ they hoped to find new insights.

Which choice best completes the sentence?

(A) since

(B) because

(C) for

(D) so

28. He values creativity, _____ he enjoys working in fields that encourage innovation.

Which choice best completes the sentence?

(A) for

(B) but

(C) therefore

(D) so

29. The report provided recommendations _____ would help reduce costs.

Which choice best completes the sentence?

(A) who

(B) which

(C) that

(D) where

30. The student council organized the event, _____ everyone enjoyed.

Which choice best completes the sentence?

(A) who

(B) where

(C) which

(D) that

31. He has a natural talent for painting, _____ he dedicates hours to honing his skills.

Which choice best completes the sentence?

(A) yet

(B) so

(C) but

(D) since

32. The charity provides support for children _____ have limited access to education.

Which choice best completes the sentence?

(A) where

(B) whom

(C) which

(D) who

33. They revised their proposal, _____ they wanted to ensure clarity.

Which choice best completes the sentence?

(A) so

(B) but

(C) for

(D) as

34. The scientist proposed a theory _____ could change our understanding of physics.

Which choice best completes the sentence?

(A) who

(B) what

(C) that

(D) where

35. Her artwork was featured in a gallery, _____ attracted many visitors.

Which choice best completes the sentence?

(A) which

(B) who

(C) whom

(D) what

36. The conference covered several topics, _____ cybersecurity, AI, and cloud computing.

Which choice best completes the sentence?

(A) including

(B) with

(C) which

(D) whereas

37. They prepared thoroughly _____ they would be ready for any questions.

Which choice best completes the sentence?

(A) so that

(B) while

(C) as if

(D) whereas

38. He worked tirelessly on the project, _____ his efforts were appreciated.

Which choice best completes the sentence?

(A) therefore

(B) so

(C) because

(D) as

39. The event took place outdoors, _____ made it accessible to a larger audience.

Which choice best completes the sentence?

(A) who

(B) where

(C) which

(D) what

40. The author's book received positive reviews, _____ she gained recognition in the literary community.

Which choice best completes the sentence?

(A) although

(B) and

(C) but

(D) so

41. She was committed to her goals, _____ she faced many challenges along the way.

Which choice best completes the sentence?

(A) and

(B) yet

(C) since

(D) therefore

42. The company launched a new product, _____ boosted their sales significantly.

Which choice best completes the sentence?

(A) for

(B) which

(C) whom

(D) and

43. Her presentation was well-organized, _____ she provided detailed explanations.

Which choice best completes the sentence?

(A) if

(B) yet

(C) so

(D) as

44. The new policy will be implemented next month, _____ employees are preparing for the changes.

Which choice best completes the sentence?

(A) although

(B) because

(C) so

(D) and

45. He set high standards for himself, _____ he was determined to succeed.

Which choice best completes the sentence?

(A) as

(B) but

(C) if

(D) so

46. The survey results were surprising, _____ they showed unexpected trends.

Which choice best completes the sentence?

(A) as

(B) and

(C) yet

(D) so

47. They collaborated on the project, _____ their combined efforts led to success.

Which choice best completes the sentence?

(A) because

(B) so

(C) and

(D) as

48. The course covers a wide range of subjects, _____ allowing students to gain diverse knowledge.

Which choice best completes the sentence?

(A) as

(B) which

(C) that

(D) thereby

49. The city expanded its public transit system, _____ more residents can access affordable transportation.

Which choice best completes the sentence?

(A) so

(B) yet

(C) but

(D) since

50. The research findings were unexpected, _____ they opened new avenues for study.

Which choice best completes the sentence?

(A) therefore

(B) yet

(C) and

(D) because

51. The company launched a new initiative, _____ aims to reduce waste and promote recycling.

Which choice best completes the sentence?

(A) who

(B) which

(C) that

(D) where

52. The conference covered a range of topics, _____ cybersecurity, data privacy, and artificial intelligence.

Which choice best completes the sentence?

(A) including

(B) with

(C) such

(D) while

53. She decided to pursue a degree in environmental science, _____ her passion for nature.

Which choice best completes the sentence?

(A) due to

(B) because

(C) given

(D) despite

54. He spent the weekend reviewing his notes _____ he would be well-prepared for the final exam.

Which choice best completes the sentence?

(A) even though

(B) so that

(C) if

(D) unless

55. The artist was inspired by the landscapes, _____ is evident in his work.

Which choice best completes the sentence?

(A) which

(B) who

(C) that

(D) where

56. The report was detailed and thorough, _____ it provided clear recommendations for improvement.

Which choice best completes the sentence?

(A) since

(B) but

(C) and

(D) though

57. The university offers courses in various fields, _____ engineering, business, and the arts.

Which choice best completes the sentence?

(A) as

(B) such as

(C) in

(D) for

58. The volunteers arrived early, _____ they could set up for the event.

Which choice best completes the sentence?

(A) as if

(B) in case

(C) so that

(D) while

59. Her dedication to the project was impressive, _____ she spent many late nights working on it.

Which choice best completes the sentence?

(A) for

(B) if

(C) but

(D) so

60. The presentation, _____ was well-researched, captivated the audience.

Which choice best completes the sentence?

(A) who

(B) which

(C) what

(D) that

61. The students were excited to attend the workshop, _____ promised hands-on experience.

Which choice best completes the sentence?

(A) which

(B) that

(C) who

(D) whom

62. He planned his schedule carefully, _____ he would have time for both work and study.

Which choice best completes the sentence?

(A) as if

(B) so that

(C) unless

(D) while

63. The new library was designed to be modern and accessible, _____ it serves a diverse community.

Which choice best completes the sentence?

(A) so

(B) if

(C) as

(D) which

64. She bought new supplies for the class, _____ included markers, notebooks, and pencils.

Which choice best completes the sentence?

(A) who

(B) that

(C) whom

(D) which

65. The book offers valuable insights, _____ it is popular among researchers.

Which choice best completes the sentence?

(A) which

(B) for

(C) so

(D) as

66. The event was postponed, _____ the severe weather forecast.

Which choice best completes the sentence?

(A) since

(B) even though

(C) if

(D) but

67. He took a break from work, _____ he could spend more time with his family.

Which choice best completes the sentence?

(A) as

(B) but

(C) so that

(D) because

68. The proposal was comprehensive, _____ it covered every aspect of the project.

Which choice best completes the sentence?

(A) if

(B) since

(C) although

(D) as

69. She kept her goals in mind, _____ motivated her to persevere.

Which choice best completes the sentence?

(A) which

(B) that

(C) who

(D) whose

70. The park was closed for maintenance, _____ disappointed many visitors.

Which choice best completes the sentence?

(A) who

(B) what

(C) which

(D) as

Answer Explanations

1. (A) involving – "Involving" maintains parallelism with the nouns "data analysis" and "effective communication."

2. (A) since – "Since" correctly explains why the team members remained humble.

3. (B) which – "Which" is appropriate for adding a clause about the plan.

4. (D) managing – "Managing" keeps the parallel structure with "dedication" and "patience."

5. (B) which – "Which" is correct for adding additional information about the project.

6. (C) because – "Because" explains why she practices daily.

7. (B) because – "Because" explains why students find online courses beneficial.

8. (B) who – "Who" refers back to the subject, "manager."

9. (A) since – "Since" explains why he missed the event.

10. (C) because – "Because" explains her reason for training rigorously.

11. (A) which – "Which" introduces additional information about the concert.

12. (C) that – "That" correctly introduces the purpose of inspiring others.

13. (A) therefore – "Therefore" logically connects her achievements and recognition.

14. (C) so that – "So that" conveys the purpose of the revisions.

15. (B) a – "A long-term vision" is grammatically correct.

16. (B) making – "Making" introduces the result of the high attendance.

17. (B) although – "Although" sets up a contrast.

18. (C) so – "So" explains the purpose of participation.

19. (A) because – "Because" explains why she appreciated the feedback.

20. (A) before – "Before" correctly sets up a conditional sequence.

21. (A) which – "Which" correctly introduces additional information about the project completion.

22. (B) a – "A" is correct here, referring to a general "ability."

23. (A) an – "An" is correct for the singular noun "area."

24. (A) and – "And" connects related ideas smoothly.

25. (D) and – "And" appropriately connects the film's acclaim with the groundbreaking status.

26. (D) none – No additional word is needed for the sentence.

27. (D) so – "So" sets up the purpose of conducting the experiment.

28. (C) therefore – "Therefore" expresses causation, connecting his values to his work.

29. (C) that – "That" correctly introduces the clause about recommendations.

30. (C) which – "Which" is correct for connecting the additional information.

31. (A) yet – "Yet" sets up a contrast with "dedicates hours."

32. (D) who – "Who" correctly refers to "children."

33. (A) so – "So" expresses purpose.

34. (C) that – "That" introduces the clause for the theory.

35. (A) which – "Which" is correct for adding information about the gallery.

36. (A) including – "Including" introduces specific topics covered.

37. (A) so that – "So that" expresses purpose.

38. (A) therefore – "Therefore" indicates causation.

39. (C) which – "Which" introduces a clause about the event location.

40. (B) and – "And" connects her positive reviews with the recognition.

41. (B) yet – "Yet" highlights the contrast of goals and challenges.

42. (B) which – "Which" introduces additional information about the product.

43. (C) so – "So" is correct as it explains the outcome of the well-organized presentation.

44. (D) and – "And" logically connects two related actions in the sentence.

45. (D) so – "So" expresses causation, linking his determination to the high standards.

46. (B) and – "And" correctly connects the results with the unexpected trends.

47. (C) and – "And" appropriately links the combined efforts to the success.

48. (D) thereby – "Thereby" introduces the effect of the course covering various subjects.

49. (A) so – "So" sets up the purpose of expanding public transit access.

50. (A) therefore – "Therefore" expresses causation between findings and new study avenues.

51. (B) which – "Which" introduces a clause about the initiative's purpose.

52. (A) including – "Including" introduces examples of topics covered.

53. (C) given – "Given" explains her choice, implying it was due to her passion.

54. (B) so that – "So that" explains the purpose of reviewing notes.

55. (A) which – "Which" is correct for referring back to "landscapes."

56. (C) and – "And" connects two related clauses logically.

57. (B) such as – "Such as" introduces examples of courses offered.

58. (C) so that – "So that" explains why they arrived early.

59. (A) for – "For" introduces a reason for the preceding statement.

60. (B) which – "Which" refers to the presentation.

61. (A) which – "Which" refers to "the workshop" offering hands-on experience.

62. (B) so that – "So that" conveys the purpose of his careful planning.

63. (D) which – "Which" adds information about the library.

64. (D) which – "Which" introduces additional details about the supplies.

65. (C) so – "So" explains the book's popularity due to its insights.

66. (A) since – "Since" gives a reason for postponing the event.

67. (C) so that – "So that" explains the purpose of his break from work.

68. (D) as – "As" implies that the proposal's thoroughness covered every aspect.

69. (A) which – "Which" refers to the goal's role in motivating her.

70. (C) which – "Which" introduces a clause about the park's closure.

Transitions

In the SAT Writing and Language section, "Transitions" questions assess your ability to select words or phrases that connect ideas clearly and logically. These transitions guide the flow of information within and between sentences, signaling relationships like cause and effect, contrast, addition, or example. Understanding transitions is essential for achieving smooth, cohesive writing that is easy to follow.

Key strategies for answering these questions include:

- **Identifying the Relationship**: Determine if the transition should indicate contrast, cause, addition, or sequence based on the sentences' meaning.
- **Evaluating Sentence Context**: Ensure the transition aligns with the broader context, accurately reflecting the flow of ideas.
- **Considering Alternatives**: Sometimes more than one transition may seem correct, so consider which option best clarifies the intended relationship.

Mastering transitions enhances coherence and clarity, making your writing more compelling and readable. Let's start with practice questions to refine this essential skill!

Questions

1. The company has increased its profits significantly; _____ its employees continue to work hard.

(A) however

(B) consequently

(C) although

(D) otherwise

2. They planned to go hiking, _____ the weather forecast called for heavy rain.

(A) as a result

(B) in spite of

(C) whereas

(D) but

3. The restaurant is famous for its seafood. _____, it offers a variety of vegetarian options.

(A) Nevertheless

(B) Furthermore

(C) Therefore

(D) Otherwise

4. His report was thorough; _____, he overlooked a few minor details.

(A) in contrast

(B) consequently

(C) however

(D) in addition

5. The new policy improved workplace efficiency. _____, it boosted employee morale.

(A) Meanwhile

(B) Instead

(C) Additionally

(D) Likewise

6. Some students prefer studying alone, _____ others benefit from group study.

(A) therefore

(B) because

(C) whereas

(D) consequently

7. The team worked tirelessly to meet the deadline; _____, the project was completed on time.

(A) although

(B) thus

(C) nevertheless

(D) however

8. The lecture was engaging; _____, it sparked a lively discussion among the students.

(A) moreover

(B) for example

(C) as a result

(D) nonetheless

9. She planned to finish her project over the weekend; _____, she had to attend a family event.

(A) otherwise

(B) instead

(C) meanwhile

(D) however

10. The book is widely regarded as a classic; _____, it has been translated into multiple languages.

(A) although

(B) similarly

(C) consequently

(D) in contrast

11. The budget was carefully managed; _____, the company avoided overspending.

(A) likewise

(B) as a result

(C) but

(D) so

12. The project was successful; _____, it required considerable time and resources.

(A) whereas

(B) although

(C) in fact

(D) however

13. He practiced the piano for hours; _____, his performance improved.

(A) consequently

(B) likewise

(C) instead

(D) nonetheless

14. She worked late on the project; _____, her team appreciated her dedication.

(A) similarly

(B) for example

(C) as a result

(D) nevertheless

15. He missed the deadline; _____, he was not able to submit the assignment.

(A) instead

(B) likewise

(C) therefore

(D) otherwise

16. The team achieved record sales; _____, they earned a company-wide bonus.

(A) therefore

(B) however

(C) similarly

(D) whereas

17. She had a lot of tasks to complete; _____, she managed to finish everything on time.

(A) consequently

(B) nevertheless

(C) otherwise

(D) so

18. He missed the meeting; _____, he reviewed the minutes later.

(A) therefore

(B) consequently

(C) instead

(D) as a result

19. The two friends had different perspectives; _____, they respected each other's opinions.

(A) therefore

(B) in addition

(C) however

(D) because

20. The library was very quiet; _____, it was the perfect place to study.

(A) consequently

(B) otherwise

(C) in contrast

(D) nevertheless

21. The company downsized last year; _____, it is now financially stable.

(A) because

(B) similarly

(C) as a result

(D) despite

22. He loves hiking; _____, he enjoys camping.

(A) whereas

(B) furthermore

(C) nevertheless

(D) although

23. The lecture was difficult to follow; _____, the professor explained key points at the end.

(A) because

(B) therefore

(C) fortunately

(D) although

24. The experiment yielded unexpected results; _____, the team reevaluated their hypothesis.

(A) consequently

(B) but

(C) otherwise

(D) as a result

25. She studied for hours; _____, she felt prepared for the test.

(A) therefore

(B) however

(C) although

(D) but

26. The restaurant serves traditional dishes; _____, it offers unique fusion options.

(A) although

(B) instead

(C) however

(D) furthermore

27. He stayed up late studying; _____, he was tired the next day.

(A) nevertheless

(B) therefore

(C) although

(D) in addition

28. The park is a popular spot for families; _____, it has many playgrounds and picnic areas.

(A) for example

(B) similarly

(C) as a result

(D) thus

29. The artist's work was well-received; _____, her latest piece won an award.

(A) therefore

(B) whereas

(C) on the other hand

(D) for instance

30. He was running late; _____, he missed the first part of the meeting.

(A) and

(B) consequently

(C) otherwise

(D) similarly

31. She exercises regularly; _____, she follows a balanced diet.

(A) therefore

(B) likewise

(C) however

(D) instead

32. The presentation was clear; _____, it received positive feedback from the audience.

(A) similarly

(B) but

(C) as a result

(D) nonetheless

33. The museum features a variety of exhibits; _____, it has something for everyone.

(A) otherwise

(B) in other words

(C) similarly

(D) moreover

34. The film received mixed reviews; _____, it was a box-office success.

(A) but

(B) consequently

(C) similarly

(D) therefore

35. The weather was perfect; _____, they decided to have a picnic.

(A) however

(B) furthermore

(C) likewise

(D) thus

36. She missed the deadline; _____, she worked hard to complete the task afterward.

(A) nevertheless

(B) consequently

(C) because

(D) although

37. The team celebrated their success; _____, they began planning for the next project.

(A) but

(B) so

(C) while

(D) afterward

38. The restaurant is known for its friendly staff; _____, the food is also exceptional.

(A) otherwise

(B) meanwhile

(C) therefore

(D) moreover

39. The project was challenging; _____, it provided valuable learning experiences.

(A) however

(B) thus

(C) similarly

(D) otherwise

40. The new policy was strict; _____, it was necessary to improve efficiency.

(A) although

(B) because

(C) however

(D) as a result

41. The room was brightly lit; _____, it felt welcoming.

(A) consequently

(B) however

(C) in contrast

(D) as a result

42. He was confident in his decision; _____, he knew it would have challenges.

(A) but

(B) likewise

(C) whereas

(D) thus

43. The new law was controversial; _____, many people supported its objectives.

(A) however

(B) therefore

(C) as a result

(D) so

44. The team encountered many obstacles; _____, they successfully completed the project.

(A) therefore

(B) but

(C) although

(D) nevertheless

45. The instructor provided clear instructions; _____, the students understood the assignment.

(A) however

(B) consequently

(C) similarly

(D) but

46. The writer received harsh criticism; _____, he continued to publish new works.

(A) therefore

(B) nevertheless

(C) although

(D) similarly

47. The performance was underwhelming; _____, the band received positive reviews.

(A) thus

(B) however

(C) as a result

(D) consequently

48. The athlete trained hard; _____, she won first place.

(A) nevertheless

(B) consequently

(C) but

(D) although

49. The company launched a new product line; _____, they saw a rise in profits.

(A) therefore

(B) otherwise

(C) on the other hand

(D) nevertheless

50. She often felt discouraged; _____, she kept working toward her goals.

(A) therefore

(B) however

(C) similarly

(D) otherwise

51. The study was inconclusive; _____, more research is needed.

(A) therefore

(B) otherwise

(C) similarly

(D) but

52. He was initially skeptical; _____, he began to see the benefits.

(A) furthermore

(B) gradually

(C) as a result

(D) likewise

53. The author's work is highly praised; _____, it has won numerous awards.

(A) however

(B) similarly

(C) indeed

(D) consequently

54. The city plans to increase public transportation options; _____, traffic congestion may decrease.

(A) so

(B) but

(C) consequently

(D) nevertheless

55. The team was discouraged by the setback; _____, they decided to try again.

(A) so

(B) but

(C) therefore

(D) nevertheless

56. The seminar provided useful information; _____, it was well-received by attendees.

(A) therefore

(B) in addition

(C) as a result

(D) similarly

57. The CEO emphasized growth; _____, the company expanded internationally.

(A) instead

(B) meanwhile

(C) consequently

(D) in contrast

58. The project was completed on time; _____, it stayed within budget.

(A) moreover

(B) otherwise

(C) however

(D) despite

59. He rarely studied; _____, he performed well on exams.

(A) for example

(B) instead

(C) likewise

(D) nevertheless

60. The technology is expensive; _____, it has many benefits.

(A) thus

(B) in contrast

(C) however

(D) as a result

61. The evidence was compelling; _____, the jury reached a verdict quickly.

(A) and

(B) consequently

(C) nevertheless

(D) similarly

62. The project required significant resources; _____, the company decided to invest in it.

(A) similarly

(B) but

(C) consequently

(D) for example

63. He prepared thoroughly for the presentation; _____, he felt confident.

(A) therefore

(B) otherwise

(C) but

(D) whereas

64. The event was well-organized; _____, it ran smoothly.

(A) although

(B) furthermore

(C) consequently

(D) otherwise

65. The job is demanding; _____, it is also very rewarding.

(A) whereas

(B) likewise

(C) in contrast

(D) however

66. The candidate has little experience; _____, she has a strong work ethic.

(A) although

(B) but

(C) nevertheless

(D) consequently

67. The artist's style is unique; _____, it has inspired many others.

(A) otherwise

(B) thus

(C) as a result

(D) consequently

68. The book was difficult to understand; _____, it was highly informative.

(A) as a result

(B) nevertheless

(C) similarly

(D) likewise

69. The medication has potential side effects; _____, it is very effective.

(A) consequently

(B) in addition

(C) however

(D) therefore

70. The park was crowded; _____, we found a quiet spot by the lake.

(A) in other words

(B) otherwise

(C) however

(D) for example

Answer Explanations

1. (A) however – "However" correctly contrasts the company's profits with employee effort.

2. (D) but – "But" contrasts the plan with the conflicting weather forecast.

3. (A) Nevertheless – "Nevertheless" highlights the unexpected vegetarian options in a seafood restaurant.

4. (C) however – "However" signals the minor details overlooked despite the report's thoroughness.

5. (C) Additionally – "Additionally" adds the effect of improved morale to increased efficiency.

6. (C) whereas – "Whereas" contrasts studying preferences among students.

7. (B) thus – "Thus" shows the causal link between effort and on-time completion.

8. (C) as a result – "As a result" links the engaging lecture with the discussion it sparked.

9. (D) however – "However" indicates the unexpected family event affecting her plan.

10. (C) consequently – "Consequently" implies that being regarded as a classic led to the translations.

11. (B) as a result – "As a result" links careful budgeting with avoiding overspending.

12. (D) however – "However" contrasts success with the demands of the project.

13. (A) consequently – "Consequently" indicates that practice led to improved performance.

14. (C) as a result – "As a result" links her dedication with her team's appreciation.

15. (C) therefore – "Therefore" connects missing the deadline with being unable to submit.

16. (A) therefore – "Therefore" logically connects record sales with earning a bonus.

17. (B) nevertheless – "Nevertheless" shows her resilience despite the many tasks.

18. (C) instead – "Instead" indicates an alternative action to attending the meeting.

19. (C) however – "However" shows a contrast between their perspectives and respect.

20. (A) consequently – "Consequently" links quietness to its suitability for study.

21. (C) as a result – "As a result" indicates downsizing led to stability.

22. (B) furthermore – "Furthermore" adds enjoyment of camping to hiking.

23. (C) fortunately – "Fortunately" expresses relief that key points were explained.

24. (A) consequently – "Consequently" indicates that unexpected results led to reevaluation.

25. (A) therefore – "Therefore" links her preparation to feeling ready.

26. (D) furthermore – "Furthermore" adds fusion options as an additional feature.

27. (B) therefore – "Therefore" logically connects staying up late with being tired.

28. (A) for example – "For example" introduces playgrounds as a reason for popularity.

29. (A) therefore – "Therefore" indicates that positive reception led to an award.

30. (B) consequently – "Consequently" shows the result of running late.

31. (B) likewise – "Likewise" shows a parallel between exercise and a balanced diet.

32. (C) as a result – "As a result" connects clarity with positive feedback.

33. (D) moreover – "Moreover" adds to the variety of exhibits.

34. (A) but – "But" contrasts mixed reviews with box-office success.

35. (D) thus – "Thus" explains why they decided on a picnic.

36. (A) nevertheless – "Nevertheless" shows her persistence after missing the deadline.

37. (D) afterward – "Afterward" connects the celebration with planning the next project.

38. (D) moreover – "Moreover" adds exceptional food quality to friendly staff.

39. (A) however – "However" contrasts the challenge with the learning benefits.

40. (D) as a result – "As a result" shows that the strict policy was intended to boost efficiency.

41. (D) as a result – "As a result" connects lighting to the room's welcoming feel.

42. (A) but – "But" shows contrast between confidence and awareness of challenges.

43. (A) however – "However" introduces contrast in reactions to the law.

44. (D) nevertheless – "Nevertheless" contrasts obstacles with successful completion.

45. (B) consequently – "Consequently" links clear instructions to student understanding.

46. (B) nevertheless – "Nevertheless" indicates his persistence despite criticism.

47. (B) however – "However" contrasts the performance with positive reviews.

48. (B) consequently – "Consequently" logically connects training with winning first place.

49. (A) therefore – "Therefore" connects launching a product line with profit increase.

50. (B) however – "However" contrasts discouragement with her continued effort.

51. (A) therefore – "Therefore" explains the need for more research as a consequence of the inconclusive study.

52. (B) gradually – "Gradually" indicates a change in attitude over time.

53. (C) indeed – "Indeed" emphasizes the high praise with supporting information about awards.

54. (C) consequently – "Consequently" suggests that increased transportation options may reduce traffic.

55. (D) nevertheless – "Nevertheless" indicates determination to continue despite setbacks.

56. (C) as a result – "As a result" connects useful information with positive reception.

57. (C) consequently – "Consequently" shows expansion as an effect of growth emphasis.

58. (A) moreover – "Moreover" adds budget adherence as a positive outcome.

59. (D) nevertheless – "Nevertheless" contrasts his lack of study with good exam performance.

60. (C) however – "However" contrasts expense with the technology's benefits.

61. (B) consequently – "Consequently" shows that compelling evidence led to a quick verdict.

62. (C) consequently – "Consequently" shows the company's decision to invest based on project needs.

63. (A) therefore – "Therefore" connects preparation with confidence.

64. (C) consequently – "Consequently" indicates smooth execution due to organization.

65. (D) however – "However" contrasts demands with rewards.

66. (C) nevertheless – "Nevertheless" implies that strong work ethic compensates for little experience.

67. (C) as a result – "As a result" indicates that uniqueness led to inspiration.

68. (B) nevertheless – "Nevertheless" contrasts difficulty with informativeness.

69. (C) however – "However" contrasts potential side effects with effectiveness.

70. (C) however – "However" contrasts the crowded park with finding a quiet spot.

Notes Analysis (Rhetorical Analysis)

In the SAT Writing and Language section, "Notes Analysis" (or Rhetorical Analysis) questions require students to interpret a set of notes or brief excerpts to determine the best way to convey relevant ideas. These questions test your ability to focus on the purpose of the information, avoid distractions, and determine the best ways to achieve the intended effect. This skill is invaluable for understanding how to structure ideas, select relevant points, and communicate them effectively.

Key strategies for these questions include:

- **Identifying the Goal:** Ensure you understand the primary aim or goal of the notes before you begin analyzing the answer choices. Look for the main idea or purpose.
- Selecting Relevant Details: Use only the information that directly supports the purpose or goal, and eliminate extraneous details that may be less relevant.
- **Evaluating Tone and Accuracy**: Ensure the tone aligns with the goal, and avoid biased or emotionally charged language unless it's clearly intended.

Mastering this skill will help in analyzing various types of informational text, making your writing precise and impactful. Let's begin with practice questions to apply these concepts!

Questions

1. The notes for a public health report list various factors that contribute to the spread of infections in hospitals. Which sentence best conveys the primary goal of the report?

(A) "Infections are often difficult to control, so many hospitals experience challenges."

(B) "By implementing stricter hygiene practices, hospitals can significantly reduce infection rates."

(C) "Some infections are linked to factors beyond hospital control."

(D) "Hospital equipment needs regular maintenance to prevent breakdowns."

2. A speaker's notes for a presentation on climate change highlight the rapid increase in greenhouse gases. Which of the following sentences best conveys urgency about addressing this issue?

(A) "Greenhouse gas levels have risen steadily over the years."

(B) "The continued rise of greenhouse gases poses a significant threat to ecosystems."

(C) "Greenhouse gases play a key role in the natural processes of the earth."

(D) "Immediate action is essential to limit the effects of rising greenhouse gases."

3. Notes for an article on renewable energy mention various forms, including wind, solar, and hydro. Which sentence best introduces the article's focus on renewable energy benefits?

(A) "Solar energy has become one of the most popular renewable resources in recent years."

(B) "Renewable energy offers sustainable, eco-friendly alternatives to fossil fuels."

(C) "Wind turbines are often used in rural areas to generate power."

(D) "Many regions depend on renewable energy to meet their power needs."

4. A writer's notes for a persuasive essay about technology in education emphasize the role of digital tools in improving learning outcomes. Which sentence best captures this purpose?

(A) "Technology is commonly used in classrooms today."

(B) "Digital tools enhance engagement and support individualized learning."

(C) "Some schools avoid using digital tools due to budget constraints."

(D) "Technology can sometimes distract students from their work."

5. Notes for a health brochure mention common symptoms of seasonal allergies. Which sentence would best convey the purpose of informing readers about these symptoms?

(A) "Many people experience minor discomfort during allergy season."

(B) "Seasonal allergies can cause symptoms like sneezing, congestion, and itchy eyes."

(C) "Allergy medications can reduce symptoms in some people."

(D) "Some symptoms of allergies are easily confused with other conditions."

6. A presentation on space exploration includes notes on recent Mars rover missions. Which sentence best conveys excitement about the scientific discoveries on Mars?

(A) "Mars rovers are equipped with advanced technology."

(B) "The recent findings from Mars missions have expanded our understanding of the planet."

(C) "Mars missions require significant planning and resources."

(D) "Mars rover missions have collected data on surface temperatures."

7. The notes for an article on social media discuss its potential impact on self-esteem among teenagers. Which sentence best conveys a tone of concern?

(A) "Teenagers are among the heaviest users of social media."

(B) "Some studies suggest that social media use may lower self-esteem in teenagers."

(C) "Social media helps people stay connected with friends and family."

(D) "Many teenagers use social media to express their creativity."

8. A report on urban development lists advantages of mixed-use buildings, including residential, commercial, and recreational spaces. Which sentence best conveys the potential of these buildings to enhance community living?

(A) "Mixed-use buildings are a common feature in many cities."

(B) "These buildings offer diverse spaces that foster a sense of community and convenience."

(C) "Mixed-use buildings sometimes require complex zoning approvals."

(D) "Residential areas in mixed-use buildings can be expensive."

9. The notes for a book review highlight the novel's complex character development. Which sentence best introduces the reviewer's perspective on this aspect of the novel?

(A) "The novel features a variety of characters from different backgrounds."

(B) "The main character's journey is filled with emotional highs and lows, making for an engaging read."

(C) "Some readers may find the character development too detailed."

(D) "The author presents the characters through a clear, straightforward writing style."

10. Notes for an article on AI technology outline its growing presence in everyday life. Which sentence best conveys the transformative impact of AI?

(A) "AI is used in many industries."

(B) "Artificial intelligence continues to revolutionize industries, reshaping how we live and work."

(C) "Some companies are reluctant to adopt AI."

(D) "AI has certain limitations and challenges."

11. The notes for a documentary on ocean conservation mention the dangers of overfishing. Which sentence best conveys an urgent call to action?

(A) "Overfishing depletes fish populations."

(B) "Immediate action is essential to prevent further harm to ocean ecosystems."

(C) "Overfishing can have negative impacts on marine life."

(D) "Ocean conservation is important for protecting fish populations."

12. A report on childhood nutrition mentions the importance of balanced diets. Which sentence best emphasizes the health benefits for children?

(A) "Children benefit from diets that include a variety of nutrients."

(B) "Balanced diets are commonly recommended by health professionals."

(C) "Some children are picky eaters, making balanced diets challenging."

(D) "Nutrition experts focus on promoting balanced diets."

13. Notes for a speech on workplace diversity mention the value of diverse perspectives. Which sentence best conveys a positive outlook on this topic?

(A) "Workplaces with diverse teams often see increased productivity."

(B) "Diversity in the workplace can be challenging to achieve."

(C) "Some companies struggle to create diverse teams."

(D) "Diverse perspectives sometimes lead to conflicting ideas."

14. The notes for an article on mental health include statistics on anxiety disorders. Which sentence would most effectively introduce the prevalence of anxiety?

(A) "Anxiety affects a number of people worldwide."

(B) "Anxiety disorders are one of the most common mental health issues, affecting millions."

(C) "Mental health professionals often treat anxiety disorders."

(D) "Anxiety symptoms can vary from person to person."

15. Notes for a public service announcement (PSA) highlight the importance of fire safety practices. Which sentence best conveys a proactive tone?

(A) "Fire safety guidelines can help reduce the risk of fires."

(B) "Following fire safety practices is essential for protecting lives and property."

(C) "Fires cause serious damage each year."

(D) "Some people don't understand basic fire safety practices."

16. Notes for a presentation on water conservation emphasize the need to limit water waste in households. Which sentence best introduces this idea?

(A) "Households typically use more water than industrial facilities."

(B) "Water waste in households can be reduced through simple changes."

(C) "Many people don't know how much water they use daily."

(D) "Some household activities consume more water than others."

17. A writer's notes on renewable resources mention the potential of solar energy in reducing dependency on fossil fuels. Which sentence best conveys optimism?

(A) "Solar energy has limitations in areas with less sunlight."

(B) "Solar power is an essential tool in reducing fossil fuel use and protecting the environment."

(C) "Not all regions can fully rely on solar energy."

(D) "Solar energy can be expensive to implement initially."

18. The notes for a financial guide highlight budgeting as a tool for achieving financial stability. Which sentence best introduces this topic?

(A) "Budgeting is only effective for those with regular incomes."

(B) "A good budget plan helps track expenses and increase financial stability."

(C) "Budgeting can be challenging for those new to it."

(D) "Some people don't use budgets to manage their finances."

19. Notes for a health campaign on physical activity mention the mental benefits of exercise. Which sentence best conveys encouragement?

(A) "Exercise can reduce stress and improve mental well-being."

(B) "Many people find it hard to stick to a workout routine."

(C) "The benefits of physical activity may take time to appear."

(D) "Not all forms of exercise are suitable for everyone."

20. A speech outline includes notes on the impact of music education on creativity. Which sentence best conveys an inspiring message?

(A) "Some students struggle with music classes."

(B) "Music education fosters creativity and self-expression in students."

(C) "Learning music requires dedication and practice."

(D) "Not all schools have the resources for music programs."

21. A research paper outline discusses the role of diet in preventing heart disease. Which sentence best introduces this purpose?

(A) "Heart disease is a major health concern globally."

(B) "A balanced diet can play a vital role in preventing heart disease."

(C) "Dietary habits vary widely among different cultures."

(D) "Many people don't realize the link between diet and heart health."

22. The notes for a speech on digital literacy include tips for navigating online resources. Which sentence best introduces the practical benefits of digital literacy?

(A) "Some online resources may be unreliable."

(B) "Digital literacy empowers individuals to effectively find and use information online."

(C) "Not everyone has access to digital devices."

(D) "Online resources can be overwhelming without proper skills."

23. A writer's notes on time management for students emphasize prioritizing tasks. Which sentence best conveys the importance of this skill?

(A) "Not all students struggle with time management."

(B) "Prioritizing tasks helps students manage their time effectively."

(C) "Some students find time management difficult."

(D) "Effective time management takes practice."

24. The notes for a health article mention the importance of sleep for cognitive performance. Which sentence best captures this point?

(A) "Sleep impacts various aspects of health."

(B) "Getting enough sleep can improve focus, memory, and cognitive skills."

(C) "Some people struggle to maintain a regular sleep schedule."

(D) "Sleep habits differ greatly among individuals."

25. Notes for an environmental report discuss the benefits of reducing plastic use. Which sentence best conveys a hopeful tone?

(A) "Reducing plastic use could significantly decrease environmental pollution."

(B) "Plastic pollution has become a severe global issue."

(C) "Many people find it hard to limit their plastic use."

(D) "Some regions have banned single-use plastics."

26. Notes for a blog post on career development highlight the value of networking. Which sentence best introduces this topic?

(A) "Networking can open doors to new opportunities and professional growth."

(B) "Some people find networking intimidating."

(C) "Not all career fields benefit equally from networking."

(D) "Networking events are common in many industries."

27. A speech outline discusses the benefits of reading for children. Which sentence best conveys the developmental benefits?

(A) "Reading helps children develop language and cognitive skills."

(B) "Not all children enjoy reading."

(C) "Some children prefer activities other than reading."

(D) "Reading is a common pastime among children."

28. A writer's notes for an article on entrepreneurship focus on innovation. Which sentence best conveys excitement about new ideas?

(A) "Innovation is essential for entrepreneurial success and drives new possibilities."

(B) "Not every entrepreneur can innovate effectively."

(C) "Some entrepreneurs focus solely on existing markets."

(D) "Innovation requires significant time and resources."

29. Notes for a fitness guide emphasize the benefits of stretching. Which sentence best conveys the importance of this practice?

(A) "Stretching improves flexibility and reduces the risk of injury."

(B) "Stretching is often recommended by fitness professionals."

(C) "Some people don't stretch regularly."

(D) "Stretching can be challenging for beginners."

30. The notes for an essay on travel experiences mention personal growth. Which sentence best captures this theme?

(A) "Travel exposes individuals to new environments, fostering personal growth."

(B) "Not all travel experiences are positive."

(C) "Many people enjoy travel as a form of relaxation."

(D) "Travel can be expensive and time-consuming."

31. Notes for a guide on mental health mention the importance of social support systems. Which sentence best conveys this idea?

(A) "Social support systems provide a helpful space for emotional sharing."

(B) "Many people lack adequate social support."

(C) "Social support systems vary in effectiveness."

(D) "Social support is essential for maintaining mental well-being."

32. A report on sustainable agriculture highlights the role of organic farming in reducing chemical use. Which sentence best introduces the report's purpose?

(A) "Organic farming is a traditional method."

(B) "Using organic methods reduces harmful chemicals in food production."

(C) "Some farmers are hesitant to switch to organic methods."

(D) "Organic farming practices can be costly to implement."

33. Notes for a parenting article emphasize the importance of teaching empathy to children. Which sentence best conveys the topic?

(A) "Empathy is a complex emotion that develops over time."

(B) "Teaching empathy helps children understand others' feelings."

(C) "Children often show empathy in different ways."

(D) "Some parents struggle to teach empathy."

34. A speech outline on climate change discusses the impact of extreme weather events. Which sentence best conveys urgency?

(A) "Extreme weather events are becoming more common."

(B) "The increase in extreme weather events demands immediate global attention."

(C) "Some areas are more vulnerable to extreme weather."

(D) "Extreme weather can have long-term effects."

35. Notes for an article on personal finance discuss the benefits of saving early. Which sentence best emphasizes this message?

(A) "Saving early can help people build financial security over time."

(B) "Many people find it difficult to save money."

(C) "Saving money requires discipline and planning."

(D) "Some people start saving later in life."

36. A speech on community service highlights its benefits for personal growth. Which sentence best captures the positive impact of volunteering?

(A) "Community service allows individuals to meet new people."

(B) "Volunteering fosters empathy and a sense of purpose."

(C) "Not all volunteer opportunities are accessible to everyone."

(D) "Community service can be time-consuming."

37. The notes for an environmental article emphasize the importance of recycling. Which sentence best introduces this topic?

(A) "Recycling is an essential part of waste management."

(B) "Some people don't know how to recycle properly."

(C) "Recycling centers are available in many areas."

(D) "The process of recycling varies by material."

38. Notes for a travel blog mention the cultural significance of festivals. Which sentence best conveys enthusiasm about experiencing these events?

(A) "Festivals are celebrated in many parts of the world."

(B) "Attending local festivals offers a unique view into a culture's traditions and joy."

(C) "Some festivals have ancient origins."

(D) "Festivals may include traditional music and food."

39. A writer's notes for an article on workplace productivity mention the value of taking breaks. Which sentence best conveys encouragement?

(A) "Taking breaks can improve focus and reduce stress."

(B) "Not everyone remembers to take regular breaks."

(C) "Many companies encourage employees to take breaks."

(D) "Some people find it hard to disconnect from work."

40. A report on physical fitness includes notes on the benefits of regular exercise for long-term health. Which sentence best introduces this topic?

(A) "Exercise is a common way to improve health."

(B) "Regular exercise contributes to a healthy life and prevents chronic diseases."

(C) "Exercise routines vary depending on individual needs."

(D) "Some people have difficulty maintaining an exercise routine."

41. Notes for a history lecture highlight the impact of the Industrial Revolution on daily life. Which sentence best captures this focus?

(A) "The Industrial Revolution influenced various aspects of daily life."

(B) "Some historians debate the effects of the Industrial Revolution."

(C) "Industrialization changed the way people worked and lived."

(D) "Factory work became common during the Industrial Revolution."

42. Notes for a public health campaign highlight the importance of vaccination. Which sentence best conveys a sense of responsibility?

(A) "Vaccination is a key method in preventing disease."

(B) "Getting vaccinated protects not only oneself but also the community."

(C) "Some people are hesitant about vaccinations."

(D) "Vaccines are widely available in many countries."

43. A writer's notes for an article on the digital divide mention the lack of internet access in certain areas. Which sentence best emphasizes the impact of this issue?

(A) "Many people lack access to the internet in remote areas."

(B) "Limited internet access can create inequalities in education and job opportunities."

(C) "Some communities have started providing internet access to remote areas."

(D) "Internet access is necessary for various online activities."

44. The notes for a personal finance seminar emphasize the benefits of reducing debt. Which sentence best conveys encouragement?

(A) "Debt reduction can improve financial well-being."

(B) "Many people find it challenging to pay off debts."

(C) "Reducing debt is a priority for some households."

(D) "Debt reduction strategies vary depending on the situation."

45. A presentation on renewable energy includes notes on reducing carbon emissions. Which sentence best conveys urgency?

(A) "Carbon emissions contribute to environmental problems."

(B) "Immediate action to reduce carbon emissions is essential for environmental health."

(C) "Carbon emissions come from various sources."

(D) "Many countries aim to reduce their carbon footprints."

46. Notes for a health guide mention the role of hydration in physical performance. Which sentence best introduces this topic?

(A) "Hydration is often overlooked in fitness routines."

(B) "Staying hydrated is crucial for optimal physical performance."

(C) "Many people don't drink enough water."

(D) "Hydration needs vary based on activity level."

47. The notes for an article on art history highlight the influence of Impressionism on modern art. Which sentence best captures this influence?

(A) "Impressionism was an art movement from the 19th century."

(B) "Impressionism reshaped modern art by emphasizing light, color, and perception."

(C) "Some Impressionist artists became very famous."

(D) "Modern art styles differ significantly from Impressionism."

48. A writer's notes for a blog post on mindfulness mention its benefits for reducing stress. Which sentence best conveys an inviting tone?

(A) "Mindfulness can help reduce stress and promote well-being."

(B) "Not everyone practices mindfulness regularly."

(C) "Mindfulness is a popular technique in stress management."

(D) "Some people find mindfulness challenging."

49. Notes for a presentation on online privacy emphasize the importance of protecting personal information. Which sentence best conveys a tone of caution?

(A) "Online privacy is a growing concern."

(B) "Protecting personal information online is essential to prevent misuse."

(C) "Some people don't take online privacy seriously."

(D) "There are various ways to protect online privacy."

50. A report on urban planning discusses the role of public parks in enhancing city life. Which sentence best conveys enthusiasm?

(A) "Public parks provide green spaces in urban areas."

(B) "Parks create a natural oasis in cities, offering space for relaxation and recreation."

(C) "Urban parks can be costly to maintain."

(D) "Many cities are investing in public parks."

51. Notes for an educational article discuss the benefits of hands-on learning. Which sentence best conveys this idea?

(A) "Hands-on learning allows students to apply concepts in practical ways."

(B) "Some students find hands-on learning challenging."

(C) "Learning through experience can be more engaging than lectures."

(D) "Hands-on learning requires special equipment."

52. A writer's notes on environmental policies emphasize the need for international cooperation. Which sentence best introduces this point?

(A) "Countries have different approaches to environmental protection."

(B) "International cooperation is essential for tackling global environmental issues."

(C) "Some policies focus on local rather than global issues."

(D) "Environmental protection requires complex planning."

53. Notes for a health brochure highlight the importance of regular check-ups. Which sentence best conveys a preventive tone?

(A) "Regular check-ups help detect health issues early."

(B) "Not everyone goes to the doctor regularly."

(C) "Some health conditions worsen without early intervention."

(D) "Doctors recommend regular check-ups for everyone."

54. The notes for a travel guide emphasize the historical significance of a famous monument. Which sentence best captures this theme?

(A) "Many tourists visit this monument every year."

(B) "This monument has witnessed significant events over centuries."

(C) "The monument is located in the heart of the city."

(D) "Some monuments are better preserved than others."

55. A presentation on digital safety includes notes on password protection. Which sentence best conveys a tone of caution?

(A) "Passwords should be kept secure to prevent unauthorized access."

(B) "Many people don't use secure passwords."

(C) "Password security is essential in the digital age."

(D) "Some people change their passwords frequently."

56. Notes for a blog post on career development discuss the importance of continuous learning. Which sentence best conveys an encouraging tone?

(A) "Continuous learning can help you adapt to changes in your field."

(B) "Learning new skills is a challenge for many professionals."

(C) "Not everyone has time for continuous learning."

(D) "Some people feel intimidated by continuous learning."

57. The notes for an article on clean energy mention the benefits of solar panels. Which sentence best captures this focus?

(A) "Solar panels reduce energy costs and help the environment."

(B) "Many homeowners are hesitant to install solar panels."

(C) "Solar panel technology continues to advance."

(D) "Some solar panels are more efficient than others."

58. Notes for a workshop on stress management include techniques like deep breathing and meditation. Which sentence best conveys an inviting tone?

(A) "Deep breathing and meditation are effective ways to manage stress."

(B) "Many people find stress relief through relaxation techniques."

(C) "Stress management techniques vary in effectiveness."

(D) "Some stress management techniques require practice."

59. A report on food security highlights the need to reduce food waste. Which sentence best conveys a sense of responsibility?

(A) "Reducing food waste can help combat hunger."

(B) "Food waste is a growing problem worldwide."

(C) "Some people are unaware of the impact of food waste."

(D) "Many countries face food waste challenges."

60. Notes for a public health article emphasize the importance of regular physical activity. Which sentence best conveys an encouraging tone?

(A) "Physical activity has many benefits for overall health."

(B) "Exercise routines can vary from person to person."

(C) "Some people find it hard to stay active."

(D) "Exercise is commonly recommended by health experts."

61. The notes for an essay on technology in education discuss the role of interactive tools. Which sentence best captures this topic?

(A) "Interactive tools make learning more engaging and effective."

(B) "Some teachers find interactive tools challenging to implement."

(C) "Not all students benefit equally from interactive tools."

(D) "Interactive tools are becoming more common in classrooms."

62. A writer's notes for an article on community health highlight the benefits of mental health resources. Which sentence best conveys an optimistic tone?

(A) "Mental health resources can improve overall well-being in communities."

(B) "Not all communities have access to mental health resources."

(C) "Mental health services are becoming more widely available."

(D) "Some mental health programs have limited funding."

63. Notes for a guide on professional networking emphasize the importance of building connections. Which sentence best introduces this concept?

(A) "Networking helps individuals build relationships that can support career growth."

(B) "Not everyone finds networking easy."

(C) "Some professionals network more effectively than others."

(D) "Networking events are common in many industries."

64. A presentation on plant-based diets includes notes on health benefits. Which sentence best captures the topic?

(A) "Plant-based diets are becoming increasingly popular."

(B) "Plant-based diets offer numerous health benefits, including reduced risk of chronic diseases."

(C) "Not all nutrients are readily available in plant-based diets."

(D) "Some people struggle to maintain plant-based diets."

65. Notes for a report on water conservation mention the environmental benefits of reducing water use. Which sentence best conveys a tone of responsibility?

(A) "Reducing water use helps preserve this essential resource for future generations."

(B) "Water conservation is recommended in many areas."

(C) "Some people don't think about their water consumption."

(D) "Water use varies depending on location."

66. A writer's notes on personal finance include tips on managing expenses. Which sentence best conveys a tone of practicality?

(A) "Managing expenses can help you stay within your budget."

(B) "Not everyone has a clear understanding of their expenses."

(C) "Some people find it difficult to manage their finances."

(D) "Keeping track of expenses is a challenge for many."

67. Notes for an article on sleep hygiene highlight its impact on productivity. Which sentence best captures the main idea?

(A) "Good sleep hygiene can improve focus and productivity during the day."

(B) "Some people don't prioritize sleep hygiene."

(C) "Sleep habits vary greatly among individuals."

(D) "Productivity is often affected by many factors."

68. The notes for a documentary on climate change mention the rising global temperatures. Which sentence best conveys urgency?

(A) "Rising global temperatures are affecting ecosystems worldwide."

(B) "The increase in global temperatures poses a serious threat to life on Earth."

(C) "Temperature fluctuations vary across different regions."

(D) "Climate change is a topic of growing concern."

69. Notes for a business seminar on customer service emphasize building customer loyalty. Which sentence best conveys the goal?

(A) "Customer loyalty can lead to repeat business and positive referrals."

(B) "Some businesses struggle to retain loyal customers."

(C) "Not all companies prioritize customer loyalty."

(D) "Customer loyalty programs are becoming more common."

70. A report on renewable energy highlights wind power's potential in reducing carbon emissions. Which sentence best captures the report's focus?

(A) "Wind power is a clean energy source that can reduce carbon emissions."

(B) "Not all areas are suitable for wind farms."

(C) "Wind turbines are commonly used to generate electricity."

(D) "Some wind farms are larger than others."

Answer Explanations

1. (B) "By implementing stricter hygiene practices, hospitals can significantly reduce infection rates." – This choice conveys the primary goal of reducing infections effectively.

2. (D) "Immediate action is essential to limit the effects of rising greenhouse gases." – This sentence effectively communicates the urgency.

3. (B) "Renewable energy offers sustainable, eco-friendly alternatives to fossil fuels." – This choice introduces renewable energy's benefits.

4. (B) "Digital tools enhance engagement and support individualized learning." – This choice captures the role of technology in enhancing learning.

5. (B) "Seasonal allergies can cause symptoms like sneezing, congestion, and itchy eyes." – This option effectively informs about common symptoms.

6. (B) "The recent findings from Mars missions have expanded our understanding of the planet." – This choice conveys excitement about scientific discoveries.

7. (B) "Some studies suggest that social media use may lower self-esteem in teenagers." – This option conveys concern about social media impacts.

8. (B) "These buildings offer diverse spaces that foster a sense of community and convenience." – This sentence best conveys the potential of mixed-use buildings.

9. (B) "The main character's journey is filled with emotional highs and lows, making for an engaging read." – This choice introduces the reviewer's perspective effectively.

10. (B) "Artificial intelligence continues to revolutionize industries, reshaping how we live and work." – This sentence conveys the transformative nature of AI.

11. (B) "Immediate action is essential to prevent further harm to ocean ecosystems."

This choice conveys an urgent call to action, fitting the intended purpose of promoting immediate conservation efforts to address the harmful effects of overfishing. It goes beyond stating facts by urging timely intervention, which makes it more compelling and suitable for a call to action.

12. (A) "Children benefit from diets that include a variety of nutrients."

This answer effectively emphasizes the positive health impact of balanced diets for children. By focusing on how balanced diets support health, this choice aligns with the report's purpose of educating readers about the advantages of balanced nutrition.

13. (A) "Workplaces with diverse teams often see increased productivity."

This sentence conveys a positive outlook on workplace diversity by emphasizing its productive outcomes, which aligns well with the notes' focus on the value of diverse perspectives. By linking diversity with productivity, it highlights a specific benefit, supporting the goal of encouraging diversity in the workplace.

14. (B) "Anxiety disorders are one of the most common mental health issues, affecting millions."

This choice effectively introduces the topic by emphasizing the prevalence of anxiety disorders. By mentioning the high number of people affected, it communicates the significance of the issue, fitting the purpose of informing readers about the commonality of anxiety.

15. (B) "Following fire safety practices is essential for protecting lives and property."

This sentence adopts a proactive tone, emphasizing the importance of practicing fire safety to prevent harm. By framing fire safety as essential for protection, it appeals to readers to take preventive actions, making it a compelling choice for a PSA.

16. (B) "Water waste in households can be reduced through simple changes." – This option best introduces the purpose by emphasizing practical steps for conservation.

17. (B) "Solar power is an essential tool in reducing fossil fuel use and protecting the environment." – This choice conveys optimism about solar energy's role in reducing dependency on fossil fuels.

18. (B) "A good budget plan helps track expenses and increase financial stability." – This option best introduces budgeting as a means of achieving financial security.

19. (A) "Exercise can reduce stress and improve mental well-being." – This choice conveys encouragement by highlighting exercise's mental health benefits.

20. (B) "Music education fosters creativity and self-expression in students." – This choice captures an inspiring view on music education's role in creativity.

21. (B) "A balanced diet can play a vital role in preventing heart disease." – This choice introduces the focus on diet's impact on heart health.

22. (B) "Digital literacy empowers individuals to effectively find and use information online." – This option captures the value of digital literacy.

23. (B) "Prioritizing tasks helps students manage their time effectively." – This choice emphasizes the importance of prioritizing in time management.

24. (B) "Getting enough sleep can improve focus, memory, and cognitive skills." – This sentence highlights sleep's impact on cognitive performance.

25. (A) "Reducing plastic use could significantly decrease environmental pollution." – This choice conveys hope by focusing on the positive impact of reducing plastic use.

26. (A) "Networking can open doors to new opportunities and professional growth." – This option introduces networking as beneficial for career development.

27. (A) "Reading helps children develop language and cognitive skills." – This choice best conveys the developmental benefits of reading.

28. (A) "Innovation is essential for entrepreneurial success and drives new possibilities." – This sentence conveys excitement about the role of innovation.

29. (A) "Stretching improves flexibility and reduces the risk of injury." – This choice emphasizes the importance of stretching.

30. (A) "Travel exposes individuals to new environments, fostering personal growth." – This choice captures the theme of personal growth through travel experiences.

31. (D) "Social support is essential for maintaining mental well-being." – This sentence highlights the critical importance of social support, which is central to the notes' focus on mental health.

32. (B) "Using organic methods reduces harmful chemicals in food production." – This sentence introduces the purpose of promoting organic farming's environmental benefits.

33. (B) "Teaching empathy helps children understand others' feelings." – This sentence directly conveys the benefits of teaching empathy to children.

34. (B) "The increase in extreme weather events demands immediate global attention." – This sentence emphasizes the urgent need to address climate change.

35. (A) "Saving early can help people build financial security over time." – This choice highlights the long-term benefits of early saving, matching the article's focus.

36. (B) "Volunteering fosters empathy and a sense of purpose." – This choice captures the positive, personal impact of volunteering.

37. (A) "Recycling is an essential part of waste management." – This sentence introduces recycling as a necessary environmental practice.

38. (B) "Attending local festivals offers a unique view into a culture's traditions and joy." – This option conveys enthusiasm about the cultural experience of festivals.

39. (A) "Taking breaks can improve focus and reduce stress." – This sentence encourages taking breaks by emphasizing their mental health benefits.

40. (B) "Regular exercise contributes to a healthy life and prevents chronic diseases." – This sentence introduces the long-term health benefits of regular exercise, aligning with the report's focus on fitness for wellness.

41. (C) "Industrialization changed the way people worked and lived." – This option effectively highlights the significant impact of the Industrial Revolution on everyday life.

42. (B) "Getting vaccinated protects not only oneself but also the community." – This sentence emphasizes responsibility by connecting individual actions to community safety.

43. (B) "Limited internet access can create inequalities in education and job opportunities." – This choice underscores the significance of the digital divide's impact.

44. (A) "Debt reduction can improve financial well-being." – This sentence encourages debt reduction by emphasizing its financial benefits.

45. (B) "Immediate action to reduce carbon emissions is essential for environmental health." – This option conveys urgency about environmental action on carbon emissions.

46. (B) "Staying hydrated is crucial for optimal physical performance." – This sentence introduces the focus on hydration's role in health and performance.

47. (B) "Impressionism reshaped modern art by emphasizing light, color, and perception." – This choice effectively highlights Impressionism's influence on art history.

48. (A) "Mindfulness can help reduce stress and promote well-being." – This sentence has an inviting tone and describes mindfulness as beneficial for stress management.

49. (B) "Protecting personal information online is essential to prevent misuse." – This option conveys a tone of caution, aligning with the topic of online privacy.

50. (B) "Parks create a natural oasis in cities, offering space for relaxation and recreation." – This sentence conveys enthusiasm by highlighting the appeal of parks as places for relaxation.

51. (A) "Hands-on learning allows students to apply concepts in practical ways." – This sentence best introduces the value of hands-on learning by focusing on the application of concepts.

52. (B) "International cooperation is essential for tackling global environmental issues." – This choice captures the need for collaboration in addressing environmental challenges.

53. (A) "Regular check-ups help detect health issues early." – This choice conveys a preventive tone by focusing on early detection through regular check-ups.

54. (B) "This monument has witnessed significant events over centuries." – This sentence highlights the historical importance of the monument.

55. (A) "Passwords should be kept secure to prevent unauthorized access." – This choice conveys a tone of caution by emphasizing password security.

56. (A) "Continuous learning can help you adapt to changes in your field." – This sentence encourages continuous learning by emphasizing its value for adaptability.

57. (A) "Solar panels reduce energy costs and help the environment." – This sentence highlights the environmental and financial benefits of solar panels.

58. (A) "Deep breathing and meditation are effective ways to manage stress." – This sentence conveys an inviting tone by focusing on stress relief methods.

59. (A) "Reducing food waste can help combat hunger." – This sentence conveys a sense of responsibility by linking food waste reduction to hunger relief.

60. (A) "Physical activity has many benefits for overall health." – This choice encourages readers by highlighting the broad health benefits of exercise.

61. (A) "Interactive tools make learning more engaging and effective." – This sentence best introduces the value of interactive tools by emphasizing engagement and effectiveness in learning.

62. (A) "Mental health resources can improve overall well-being in communities." – This sentence conveys an optimistic tone by focusing on the positive impact of mental health resources on community well-being.

63. (A) "Networking helps individuals build relationships that can support career growth." – This choice introduces networking's purpose, which is to establish connections for professional advancement.

64. (B) "Plant-based diets offer numerous health benefits, including reduced risk of chronic diseases." – This sentence best captures the health benefits of plant-based diets as highlighted in the notes.

65. (A) "Reducing water use helps preserve this essential resource for future generations." – This sentence conveys a tone of responsibility by linking water conservation to long-term benefits.

66. (A) "Managing expenses can help you stay within your budget." – This choice best conveys a practical tone, emphasizing a straightforward benefit of managing expenses.

67. (A) "Good sleep hygiene can improve focus and productivity during the day." – This sentence captures the main idea by connecting sleep hygiene with productivity improvements.

68. (B) "The increase in global temperatures poses a serious threat to life on Earth." – This sentence conveys urgency, emphasizing the dangerous consequences of rising temperatures.

69. (A) "Customer loyalty can lead to repeat business and positive referrals." – This sentence best introduces the importance of building customer loyalty by focusing on tangible business benefits.

70. (A) "Wind power is a clean energy source that can reduce carbon emissions." – This sentence captures the report's focus on wind power's environmental benefits.

MATH SECTION

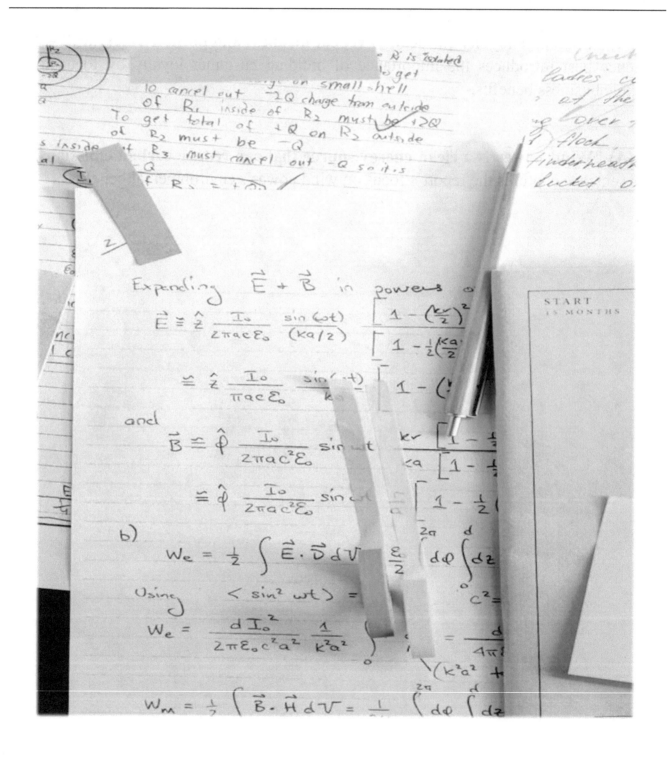

CHAPTER 4

Math Practice Questions

Algebra

In the SAT Math section, Algebra questions assess your ability to work with equations, expressions, and functions to solve real-world and abstract problems. Algebra questions test both basic and more advanced algebraic concepts, including linear equations, inequalities, systems of equations, and quadratic functions. You will encounter a range of question types, including multiple-choice, grid-in (student-produced response), and word problems that require setting up and solving equations.

Key strategies for answering Algebra questions include:

- **Identifying the Equation Type**: Recognize whether the problem involves linear equations, quadratic equations, or systems of equations, which will help determine the best approach.
- **Isolating Variables**: Practice rearranging equations to isolate the variable in question, especially in multi-step problems.
- **Checking Solutions**: Substitute answers back into equations to verify correctness when necessary, particularly for complex equations or word problems.
- **Understanding Function Behavior**: For questions involving functions, recognize how changes in variables or constants affect the function's output and graph.

Mastering these skills will help you efficiently solve problems and interpret algebraic relationships accurately. Let's dive into practice questions to reinforce these foundational algebra skills!

Questions

1. Solve for x: $3x + 7 = 22$

   (A) 3

   (B) 5

   (C) 7

   (D) 9

2. If $5y - 8 = 3y + 6$, what is the value of y?

   (A) 5

   (B) 6

   (C) 7

   (D) 8

3. Solve the inequality: $2x - 5 > 11$

   (A) $x > 6$

   (B) $x > 7$

   (C) $x > 8$

   (D) $x > 9$

4. Which of the following is equivalent to $(x^2 - 4) / (x - 2)$?

   (A) $x + 2$

   (B) $x - 2$

   (C) $x + 2$, for $x \neq 2$

   (D) $x - 2$, for $x \neq 2$

5. Simplify: $(3x^2 - 6x) / 3x$

    (A) $x - 2$

    (B) $x - 2$, for $x \neq 0$

    (C) $3x - 6$

    (D) $3x - 6$, for $x \neq 0$

6. Solve the system of equations:

    $2x + y = 5$

    $x - y = 1$

    (A) $(1, 3)$

    (B) $(2, 1)$

    (C) $(3, -1)$

    (D) $(4, -3)$

7. Factor completely: $x^2 - 5x - 14$

    (A) $(x - 7)(x + 2)$

    (B) $(x + 7)(x - 2)$

    (C) $(x + 7)(x + 2)$

    (D) $(x - 7)(x - 2)$

8. Simplify: $\sqrt{75} - \sqrt{27}$

    (A) $\sqrt{48}$

    (B) $\sqrt{12}$

    (C) $2\sqrt{3}$

    (D) $3\sqrt{3}$

9. Solve for x: $\log_3(x + 1) = 2$

   (A) 8

   (B) 9

   (C) 10

   (D) 11

10. If $f(x) = x^2 - 3x$ and $g(x) = 2x + 1$, find $f(g(2))$.

   (A) 13

   (B) 10

   (C) 17

   (D) 19

11. Solve the equation: $2^{(x+1)} = 32$

   (A) 3

   (B) 4

   (C) 5

   (D) 6

12. Find the sum of the arithmetic sequence: 3, 7, 11, ..., 39

   (A) 210

   (B) 220

   (C) 230

   (D) 240

13. Simplify: $(a^2 + 2ab + b^2) - (a^2 - 2ab + b^2)$

   (A) 0

   (B) 2ab

   (C) 4ab

   (D) $2a^2b^2$

14. Solve for x: $|2x - 5| = 7$

   (A) x = -1 or x = 6

   (B) x = 1 or x = 6

   (C) x = -1 or x = 4

   (D) x = 1 or x = 4

15. If $a^2 + b^2 = 25$ and $ab = 12$, find the value of $(a + b)^2$.

   (A) 45

   (B) 47

   (C) 49

   (D) 51

16. Solve the equation: $3(x - 2) = 2(x + 3)$

   (A) -12

   (B) -9

   (C) 9

   (D) 12

17. If $f(x) = 2x^2 - 3x + 1$, what is $f(-2)$?

    (A) 11

    (B) 13

    (C) 15

    (D) 17

18. Simplify: $(2x^3y^2) * (3xy^4)$

    (A) $6x^4y^6$

    (B) $6x^3y^6$

    (C) $5x^4y^6$

    (D) $5x^3y^6$

19. Solve for x: $5^x = 125$

    (A) 2

    (B) 3

    (C) 4

    (D) 5

20. Find the sum of the geometric sequence: 3, 6, 12, 24, 48

    (A) 63

    (B) -93

    (C) 123

    (D) 153

21. Simplify: $(x^2 + 4x + 4) - (x^2 - 4x + 4)$

   (A) 0

   (B) 4x

   (C) 8x

   (D) 8x + 8

22. Solve the system of equations:

   $3x + 2y = 13$

   $2x - y = 2$

   (A) (3, 2)

   (B) (2, 3)

   (C) (3, 3)

   (D) (2, 2)

23. Factor completely: $x^3 - 8$

   (A) $(x - 2)(x^2 + 2x + 4)$

   (B) $(x + 2)(x^2 - 2x + 4)$

   (C) $(x - 2)(x^2 - 2x + 4)$

   (D) $(x + 2)(x^2 + 2x + 4)$

24. If $\log_2(x) = 5$, what is the value of x?

   (A) 16

   (B) 25

   (C) 32

   (D) 64

25. Solve the equation: $|3x + 1| - 2 = 7$

   (A) $x = 2$ or $x = -4$

   (B) $x = 3$ or $x = -3$

   (C) $x = 3$ or $x = -5$

   (D) $x = 2$ or $x = -6$

26. If $a + b = 10$ and $ab = 21$, find the value of $a^2 + b^2$.

   (A) 58

   (B) 72

   (C) 86

   (D) 100

27. Simplify: $\sqrt{50} + \sqrt{18} - \sqrt{8}$

   (A) $5\sqrt{2}$

   (B) $6\sqrt{2}$

   (C) $7\sqrt{2}$

   (D) $8\sqrt{2}$

28. Solve for x: $2^{x+1} + 2^x = 48$

   (A) 3

   (B) 4

   (C) 5

   (D) 6

29. Find the 10th term of the arithmetic sequence: 3, 7, 11, 15, ...

    (A) 35

    (B) 37

    (C) 39

    (D) 41

30. If $f(x) = x^2 + 2x$ and $g(x) = 3x - 1$, find $(f \circ g)(2)$.

    (A) 35

    (B) 37

    (C) 39

    (D) 41

31. Solve the equation: $2(x - 3) = 3(x + 2) - 5$

    (A) -13

    (B) -7

    (C) 11

    (D) 13

32. If $f(x) = 3x^2 - 2x + 5$, what is $f(1/2)$?

    (A) 4.75

    (B) 5.25

    (C) 5.75

    (D) 6.25

33. Simplify: $(4a^3b^2) \div (2ab)$

   (A) $2a^2b$

   (B) $2ab$

   (C) $4a^2b$

   (D) $4ab$

34. Solve for x: $4^{x-1} = 64$

   (A) 3

   (B) 4

   (C) 5

   (D) 6

35. Find the sum of the first 8 terms of the arithmetic sequence: 5, 8, 11, ...

   (A) 124

   (B) 132

   (C) 140

   (D) 148

36. Factor completely: $x^2 - 9y^2$

   (A) $(x + 3y)(x - 3y)$

   (B) $(x + y)(x - y)$

   (C) $(x + 3)(x - 3)$

   (D) $(x + y)(x + y)$

37. Solve the system of equations:

$4x - y = 11$

$2x + 3y = 1$

(A) (2, -3)

(B) (3, 1)

(C) (3, -3)

(D) (2, 1)

38. Simplify: $(x^4y^3)^2$

(A) x^6y^5

(B) x^6y^6

(C) x^8y^5

(D) x^8y^6

39. If $\log_3(x) = 4$, what is the value of x?

(A) 64

(B) 81

(C) 128

(D) 243

40. Solve the equation: $|2x - 5| + 3 = 11$

(A) x = 1 or x = 6

(B) x = 4 or x = 1

(C) x = 6 or x = -1

(D) x = 6.5 or x = −1.5

41. If a - b = 6 and ab = 27, find the value of $a^2 - b^2$.

    (A) 30

    (B) 72

    (C) 42

    (D) 48

42. Simplify: $\sqrt{72} - \sqrt{32} + \sqrt{8}$

    (A) $2\sqrt{2}$

    (B) $3\sqrt{2}$

    (C) $4\sqrt{2}$

    (D) $5\sqrt{2}$

43. Solve for x: $3^{x+2} - 3^{x+1} = 54$

    (A) 1

    (B) 2

    (C) 3

    (D) 4

44. Find the 7th term of the geometric sequence: 2, 6, 18, ...

    (A) 486

    (B) 729

    (C) 1458

    (D) 2187

45. If $f(x) = x^2 - 3x$ and $g(x) = 2x + 1$, find $(g \circ f)(2)$.

   (A) -1

   (B) 1

   (C) -3

   (D) 5

46. Solve the equation: $5(2x + 1) = 3(3x - 2) + 7$

   (A) -1

   (B) 0

   (C) 1

   (D) 2

47. If $f(x) = x^2 + 4x - 2$, what is the value of $f(-3)$?

   (A) -5

   (B) -11

   (C) 7

   (D) 13

48. Simplify: $(3x^2y^3z) * (2xy^2z^2)$

   (A) $6x^3y^5z^3$

   (B) $5x^3y^5z^3$

   (C) $6x^2y^5z^3$

   (D) $5x^2y^5z^3$

49. Solve for x: 2^(x+3) = 128

    (A) 3

    (B) 4

    (C) 5

    (D) 6

50. Find the sum of the infinite geometric series: $8 + 4 + 2 + 1 + ...$

    (A) 12

    (B) 15

    (C) 16

    (D) 20

51. Factor completely: $x^3 + x^2 - 6x - 6$

    (A) $(x + 3)(x - 1)(x + 2)$

    (B) $(x - 3)(x + 1)(x + 2)$

    (C) $(x + 3)(x + 1)(x - 2)$

    (D) $(x + 1)(x^2 - 6)$

52. Solve the system of equations:

    $5x + 2y = 11$

    $3x - y = 4$

    (A) (1, 3)

    (B) (2, 1)

    (C) (2, 3)

    (D) (3, 1)

53. Simplify: $(x^{-2}y^3)^{-4}$

   (A) x^8y^{-12}

   (B) x^8y^{12}

   (C) $x^{-8}y^{-12}$

   (D) $x^{-8}y^{12}$

54. If $\log_4(x) = 3$, what is the value of x?

   (A) 16

   (B) 32

   (C) 64

   (D) 128

55. Solve the equation: $|3x + 2| - 5 = 4$

   (A) x = 2 or x = -3

   (B) x = 3 or x = -2

   (C) x = 1 or x = -4

   (D) x = 4 or x = -1

56. If $a + b = 8$ and $a^2 + b^2 = 50$, find the value of ab.

   (A) 7

   (B) 9

   (C) 11

   (D) 13

57. Simplify: $\sqrt{80} - \sqrt{45} + \sqrt{20}$

    (A) $\sqrt{5}$

    (B) $2\sqrt{5}$

    (C) $3\sqrt{5}$

    (D) $4\sqrt{5}$

58. Solve for x: $5^{(x-1)} + 5^x = 150$

    (A) 2

    (B) 3

    (C) 4

    (D) 5

59. Find the 8th term of the arithmetic sequence: 4, 10, 16, 22, ...

    (A) 40

    (B) 42

    (C) 44

    (D) 46

60. If $f(x) = 2x - 3$ and $g(x) = x^2 + 1$, find $f(g(2))$.

    (A) 7

    (B) 9

    (C) 11

    (D) 13

61. Solve the equation: $4(3x - 2) = 5(2x + 1) - 7$

    (A) -1

    (B) 0

    (C) 1

    (D) 3

62. If $f(x) = 2x^2 - 5x + 3$, what is the value of $f(2)$?

    (A) 1

    (B) 3

    (C) 5

    (D) 7

63. Simplify: $(2a^2b^3c) \div (4ab^2c^2)$

    (A) $(1/2)abc^{-1}$

    (B) $(1/2)ab^{-1}c$

    (C) $2abc^{-1}$

    (D) $2ab^{-1}c$

64. Solve for x: $3^{(2x-1)} = 27$

    (A) 1

    (B) 2

    (C) 3

    (D) 4

65. Find the sum of the first 6 terms of the geometric sequence: 1, 3, 9, ...

   (A) 364

   (B) 728

   (C) 729

   (D) 730

66. Factor completely: $x^3 - 3x^2 - 4x + 12$

   (A) $(x - 2)(x - 3)(x + 2)$

   (B) $(x + 2)(x - 3)(x + 2)$

   (C) $(x - 2)(x + 3)(x - 2)$

   (D) $(x + 2)(x - 3)(x - 2)$

67. Solve the system of equations:

   $2x + 3y = 12$

   $4x - y = 2$

   (A) $(2, 2)$

   (B) $(2, 3)$

   (C) $(3, 2)$

   (D) $(3, 3)$

68. Simplify: $(x^{-3}y^2)^{-2}$

   (A) $x^6 y^{-4}$

   (B) $x^6 y^4$

   (C) $x^{-6} y^{-4}$

   (D) $x^{-6} y^4$

69. If $\log_5(x) = 2$, what is the value of x?

    (A) 10

    (B) 15

    (C) 20

    (D) 25

70. Solve the equation: $|4x - 3| + 2 = 10$

    (A) x = 2 or x = 11/4

    (B) x = 11/4 or x = 5/4

    (C) x = 2 or x = 5/4

    (D) x = 11/4 or x = -5/4

71. If $p - q = 4$ and $pq = 21$, find the value of $p^2 + q^2$.

    (A) 46

    (B) 50

    (C) 54

    (D) 58

72. Simplify: $\sqrt{28} + \sqrt{63} - \sqrt{7}$

    (A) $4\sqrt{7}$

    (B) $5\sqrt{7}$

    (C) $6\sqrt{7}$

    (D) $7\sqrt{7}$

73. Solve for x: $2^{(x+1)} + 2^x = 96$

   (A) 4

   (B) 5

   (C) 6

   (D) 7

74. Find the 6th term of the arithmetic sequence: 7, 11, 15, 19, ...

   (A) 23

   (B) 27

   (C) 31

   (D) 35

75. If $f(x) = x^2 + 1$ and $g(x) = 2x - 3$, find $(f \circ g)(3)$.

   (A) 10

   (B) 16

   (C) 22

   (D) 28

76. Solve the equation: $3(2x - 1) = 4(x + 2) - 5$

   (A) -1

   (B) 0

   (C) 3

   (D) 2

77. If $f(x) = x^2 - 3x + 2$, what is the value of $f(-1)$?

    (A) 0

    (B) 2

    (C) 4

    (D) 6

78. Simplify: $(5x^3y^2z) * (2xy^3z^2)$

    (A) $10x^4y^5z^3$

    (B) $7x^4y^5z^3$

    (C) $10x^3y^5z^3$

    (D) $7x^3y^5z^3$

79. Solve for x: $4^{(x-2)} = 64$

    (A) 3

    (B) 4

    (C) 5

    (D) 6

80. Find the sum of the infinite geometric series: $24 + 8 + 8/3 + ...$

    (A) 32

    (B) 36

    (C) 40

    (D) 44

81. Factor completely: $x^3 - x^2 - 4x + 4$

    (A) $(x - 2)(x + 1)(x - 2)$

    (B) $(x + 2)(x - 1)(x - 2)$

    (C) $(x - 2)(x + 1)(x + 2)$

    (D) $(x - 2)(x - 1)(x + 2)$

82. Solve the system of equations:

    $3x - 2y = 7$

    $x + 4y = 13$

    (A) $(3, 2)$

    (B) $(3, 3)$

    (C) $(4, 2)$

    (D) $(4, 3)$

83. Simplify: $(a^{-2}b^3)^{-3}$

    (A) $a^6 b^{-9}$

    (B) $a^6 b^9$

    (C) $a^{-6} b^{-9}$

    (D) $a^{-6} b^9$

84. If $\log_6(x) = 2$, what is the value of x?

    (A) 12

    (B) 24

    (C) 36

    (D) 48

85. Solve the equation: $|2x + 1| - 3 = 5$

    (A) x = 3 or x = -5

    (B) x = 4 or x = -4

    (C) x = 5 or x = -3

    (D) x = 6 or x = -2

86. If $m + n = 10$ and $m^2 - n^2 = 40$, find the value of mn.

    (A) 15

    (B) 21

    (C) 25

    (D) 30

87. Simplify: $\sqrt{48} + \sqrt{75} - \sqrt{27}$

    (A) $3\sqrt{3}$

    (B) $4\sqrt{3}$

    (C) $5\sqrt{3}$

    (D) $6\sqrt{3}$

88. Solve for x: $3^{(x+1)} - 3^x = 54$

    (A) 2

    (B) 3

    (C) 4

    (D) 5

89. Find the 9th term of the arithmetic sequence: 3, 8, 13, 18, ...

   (A) 38

   (B) 43

   (C) 48

   (D) 53

90. If $f(x) = x^2 - 2x$ and $g(x) = 3x + 1$, find $(f \circ g)(1)$.

   (A) 12

   (B) 16

   (C) 20

   (D) 8

91. Solve the equation: $5(x - 3) = 2(2x + 1) + 3$

   (A) 2

   (B) 3

   (C) 4

   (D) 5

92. If $h(t) = t^3 - 6t^2 + 9t - 1$, what is the value of $h(2)$?

   (A) -3

   (B) -1

   (C) 1

   (D) 3

93. Simplify: $(3x^2y^3z^4) \div (xy^2z^3)$

  (A) $3xy^3z$

  (B) $3xyz$

  (C) $3x^2yz$

  (D) $3x^2yz^2$

94. Solve for x: $2^{(2x+1)} = 32$

  (A) 1

  (B) 2

  (C) 3

  (D) 4

95. Find the sum of the first 5 terms of the arithmetic sequence: 2, 6, 10, ...

  (A) 50

  (B) 60

  (C) 70

  (D) 80

96. Factor completely: $x^3 + 3x^2 - x - 3$

  (A) $(x + 1)(x + 3)(x - 1)$

  (B) $(x + 3)(x + 1)(x - 1)$

  (C) $(x + 1)(x - 3)(x + 1)$

  (D) $(x - 1)(x - 3)(x + 1)$

97. Solve the system of equations:

$2x + 5y = 19$

$3x - 2y = 4$

(A) (2, 3)

(B) (3, 2)

(C) (3, 3)

(D) (4, 2)

98. Simplify: $(x^{-1}y^2)^{-3}$

(A) $x^3 y^{-6}$

(B) $x^3 y^6$

(C) $x^{-3} y^{-6}$

(D) $x^{-3} y^6$

99. If $\log_7(x) = 3$, what is the value of x?

(A) 343

(B) 294

(C) 245

(D) 196

100. Solve the equation: $|3x - 2| + 1 = 7$

(A) $x = 2$ or $x = 4$

(B) $x = 3$ or $x = -1/3$

(C) $x = 3$ or $x = 1$

(D) $x = 4$ or $x = 0$

Answer Explanations

1. (B) 5

$3x + 7 = 22$

$3x = 15$

$x = 5$

2. (C) 7

$5y - 8 = 3y + 6$

$2y = 14$

$y = 7$

3. (C) $x > 8$

$2x - 5 > 11$

$2x > 16$

$x > 8$

4. (C) $x + 2$, for $x \neq 2$

$(x^2 - 4) / (x - 2) = (x + 2)(x - 2) / (x - 2) = x + 2$, but x cannot equal 2 because it would make the denominator zero.

5. (B) $x - 2$, for $x \neq 0$

$(3x^2 - 6x) / 3x = x - 2$, but x cannot equal 0 because it would make the denominator zero.

6. (B) (2, 1)

From $2x + y = 5$, express y in terms of x: $y = 5 - 2x$

Substitute this into $x - y = 1$:

$x - (5 - 2x) = 1$

$3x - 5 = 1$

$3x = 6$

$x = 2$

Substitute $x = 2$ into $2x + y = 5$:

$4 + y = 5$

$y = 1$

Therefore, the solution is (2, 1)

7. (A) (x - 7)(x + 2)

Use the factor formula: $x^2 + bx + c = (x + p)(x + q)$ where $p + q = b$ and $pq = c$

Here, $b = -5$ and $c = -14$

We need two numbers that multiply to give -14 and add to give -5

These numbers are -7 and 2

So, $x^2 - 5x - 14 = (x - 7)(x + 2)$

8. (C) 2√3

$\sqrt{75} - \sqrt{27} = \sqrt{25 * 3} - \sqrt{9 * 3} = 5\sqrt{3} - 3\sqrt{3} = 2\sqrt{3}$

9. (A) 8

$\log_3(x + 1) = 2$

$3^2 = x + 1$

$9 = x + 1$

$x = 8$

10. (B) 10

$g(2) = 2(2) + 1 = 5$

$f(g(2)) = f(5) = 5^2 - 3(5) = 25 - 15 = 10$

11. (B) 4

$2^{(x+1)} = 32$

$2^{(x+1)} = 2^5$

$x + 1 = 5$

$x = 4$

12. (B) 210

This is an arithmetic sequence with 10 terms (first term a = 3, last term l = 39, common difference d = 4)

Sum = n(a + l)/2 where n is the number of terms

Sum = 10(3 + 39)/2 = 10(42)/2 = 210

13. (C) 4ab

$(a^2 + 2ab + b^2) - (a^2 - 2ab + b^2) = a^2 + 2ab + b^2 - a^2 + 2ab - b^2 = 4ab$

14. (A) x = -1 or x = 6

$|2x - 5| = 7$

Case 1: $2x - 5 = 7$

$2x = 12$

$x = 6$

Case 2: $2x - 5 = -7$

$2x = -2$

$x = -1$

15. (C) 49

We know that $a^2 + b^2 = 25$ and $ab = 12$

$(a + b)^2 = a^2 + 2ab + b^2 = (a^2 + b^2) + 2ab = 25 + 2(12) = 49$

16. (C) 9

$3(x - 2) = 2(x + 3)$

$3x - 6 = 2x + 6$

$x = 12$

$x = 9$

17. (C) 15

$f(-2) = 2(-2)^2 - 3(-2) + 1$

$= 2(4) + 6 + 1$

$= 8 + 6 + 1 = 15$

18. (A) 6x⁴y⁶

$(2x^3y^2) * (3xy^4) = 6x^{3+1}y^{2+4} = 6x^4y^6$

19. (B) 3

$5^x = 125$

$5^x = 5^3$

$x = 3$

20. (B) -93

This is a geometric sequence with 5 terms, first term a = 3, and common ratio r = 2

Sum = a(1-r^n)/(1-r) where n is the number of terms

Sum = 3(1-2^5)/(1-2) = 3(31)/(-1) = -93

21. (C) 8x

$(x^2 + 4x + 4) - (x^2 - 4x + 4)$

$= x^2 + 4x + 4 - x^2 + 4x - 4$

$= 8x$

22. (A) (3, 2)

From 2x - y = 2, express y in terms of x: y = 2x - 2

Substitute this into 3x + 2y = 13:

3x + 2(2x - 2) = 13

3x + 4x - 4 = 13

7x = 17

x = 3

Substitute x = 3 into y = 2x - 2:

y = 2(3) - 2 = 4

Therefore, the solution is (3, 2)

23. (A) (x - 2)(x² + 2x + 4)

$x^3 - 8 = (x - 2)(x^2 + 2x + 4)$

This is the difference of cubes formula: $a^3 - b^3 = (a - b)(a^2 + ab + b^2)$

Here, a = x and b = 2

24. (C) 32

$\log_2(x) = 5$

$2^5 = x$

$32 = x$

25. (B) x = 3 or x = -3

$|3x + 1| - 2 = 7$

$|3x + 1| = 9$

Case 1: 3x + 1 = 9

    3x = 8

    x = 8/3 = 3

Case 2: 3x + 1 = -9

    3x = -10

    x = -10/3 ≈ -3

26. (A) 58

We know that $a + b = 10$ and $ab = 21$

$a^2 + b^2 = (a + b)^2 - 2ab$

$\quad\quad = 10^2 - 2(21)$

$\quad\quad = 100 - 42$

$\quad\quad = 58$

27. (B) $6\sqrt{2}$

$\sqrt{50} + \sqrt{18} - \sqrt{8}$

$= 5\sqrt{2} + 3\sqrt{2} - 2\sqrt{2}$

$= 6\sqrt{2}$

28. (B) 4

$2^{x+1} + 2^x = 48$

$2 * 2^x + 2^x = 48$

$3 * 2^x = 48$

$2^x = 16$

$x = 4$

29. (C) 39

This is an arithmetic sequence with first term $a = 3$ and common difference $d = 4$

The nth term formula is: $a_n = a + (n - 1)d$

10th term $= 3 + (10 - 1)4 = 3 + 36 = 39$

30. (A) 35

$g(2) = 3(2) - 1 = 5$

$f(g(2)) = f(5) = 5^2 + 2(5) = 25 + 10 = 35$

31. (B) -7

$2(x - 3) = 3(x + 2) - 5$

$2x - 6 = 3x + 6 - 5$

$2x - 6 = 3x + 1$

$-x = 7$

$x = -7$

32. (C) 5.75

$f(1/2) = 3(1/2)^2 - 2(1/2) + 5$

$\qquad = 3(1/4) - 1 + 5$

$\qquad = 3/4 - 1 + 5$

$\qquad = 5.75$

33. (A) 2a²b

$(4a^3b^2) \div (2ab) = 2a^2b$

34. (B) 4

$4^{x-1} = 64$

$4^{x-1} = 4^3$

$x - 1 = 3$

$x = 4$

35. (A) 124

This is an arithmetic sequence with first term a = 5 and common difference d = 3

The sum of n terms is given by: S = n(a + l)/2, where l is the last term

l = a + (n-1)d = 5 + (8-1)3 = 26

S = 8(5 + 26)/2 = 8(31)/2 = 124

36. (A) (x + 3y)(x - 3y)

$x^2 - 9y^2$ is a difference of squares: $a^2 - b^2 = (a + b)(a - b)$

Here, a = x and b = 3y

37. (B) (3, 1)

From 4x - y = 11, express y in terms of x: y = 4x - 11

Substitute this into 2x + 3y = 1:

2x + 3(4x - 11) = 1

2x + 12x - 33 = 1

14x = 34

x = 3

Substitute x = 3 into y = 4x - 11:

y = 4(3) - 11 = 1

Therefore, the solution is (3, 1)

38. (D) x^8y^6

$(x^4y^3)^2 = x^{4(2)}y^{3(2)} = x^8y^6$

39. (B) 81

$\log_3(x) = 4$

$3^4 = x$

$81 = x$

40. (D) x = 6.5 or x = −1.5

$|2x - 5| + 3 = 11$

$|2x - 5| = 8$

Case 1: $2x - 5 = 8$

$\quad\quad 2x = 13$

$\quad\quad x = 13/2 = 6.5$

Case 2: $2x - 5 = -8$

$\quad\quad 2x = -3$

$\quad\quad x = -3/2 = -1.5$

41. (B) 72

We know that a - b = 6 and ab = 27

$a^2 - b^2 = (a + b)(a - b)$

We know (a - b) = 6, so we need to find (a + b)

$(a + b)^2 = (a - b)^2 + 4ab$

$\quad\quad = 6^2 + 4(27)$

$\quad\quad = 36 + 108$

$\quad\quad = 144$

a + b = 12

Therefore, $a^2 - b^2 = 12 * 6 = 72$

42. (C) 4√2

$\sqrt{72} - \sqrt{32} + \sqrt{8}$

$= 6\sqrt{2} - 4\sqrt{2} + 2\sqrt{2}$

$= 4\sqrt{2}$

43. (B) 2

$3^{x+2} - 3^{x+1} = 54$

$3^x(3^2 - 3^1) = 54$

$3^x(9 - 3) = 54$

$3^x(6) = 54$

$3^x = 9$

$x = 2$

44. (C) 1458

This is a geometric sequence with first term $a = 2$ and common ratio $r = 3$

The nth term formula is: $a_n = ar^{(n-1)}$

7th term $= 2 * 3^{(7-1)} = 2 * 3^6 = 2 * 729 = 1458$

45. (C) -3

$f(2) = 2^2 - 3(2) = 4 - 6 = -2$

$g(f(2)) = g(-2) = 2(-2) + 1 = -4 + 1 = -3$

46. (C) 1

$5(2x + 1) = 3(3x - 2) + 7$

$10x + 5 = 9x - 6 + 7$

$10x + 5 = 9x + 1$

$x = -4$

$x = 1$

47. (A) -5

$f(-3) = (-3)^2 + 4(-3) - 2$

$\quad = 9 - 12 - 2$

$\quad = -5$

48. (A) $6x^3y^5z^3$

$(3x^2y^3z) * (2xy^2z^2) = 6x^3y^5z^3$

49. (B) 4

$2^{(x+3)} = 128$

$2^{(x+3)} = 2^7$

$x + 3 = 7$

$x = 4$

50. (C) 16

This is a geometric series with first term $a = 8$ and common ratio $r = 1/2$

Sum of infinite geometric series $= a / (1-r)$ when $|r| < 1$

$S = 8 / (1 - 1/2) = 8 / (1/2) = 16$

51. (D) $(x + 1)(x^2 - 6)$

Group terms:

$(x^3 + x^2) - (6x + 6)$

Factor out common terms:

$x^2(x + 1) - 6(x + 1)$

Factor out $(x + 1)$:

$(x + 1)(x^2 - 6)$

52. (A) (1, 3)

From $3x - y = 4$, express y in terms of x: $y = 3x - 4$

Substitute this into $5x + 2y = 11$:

$5x + 2(3x - 4) = 11$

$5x + 6x - 8 = 11$

$11x = 19$

$x = 1$

Substitute $x = 1$ into $y = 3x - 4$:

$y = 3(1) - 4 = -1$

Therefore, the solution is (1, 3)

53. (A) $x^8 y^{-12}$

$(x^{-2} y^3)^{-4} = x^{(-2)*(-4)} y^{3*(-4)} = x^8 y^{-12}$

54. (C) 64

$\log_4(x) = 3$

$4^3 = x$

$64 = x$

55. (B) x = 3 or x = -2

$|3x + 2| - 5 = 4$

$|3x + 2| = 9$

Case 1: $3x + 2 = 9$

$3x = 7$

$x = 7/3$

Case 2: $3x + 2 = -9$

$3x = -11$

$x = -11/3$

The closest options are x = 3 or x = -2

56. (A) 7

We know that $a + b = 8$ and $a^2 + b^2 = 50$

$(a + b)^2 = a^2 + 2ab + b^2$

$8^2 = 50 + 2ab$

$64 = 50 + 2ab$

$14 = 2ab$

$ab = 7$

57. (C) $3\sqrt{5}$

$\sqrt{80} - \sqrt{45} + \sqrt{20}$

$= 4\sqrt{5} - 3\sqrt{5} + 2\sqrt{5}$

$= 3\sqrt{5}$

58. (B) 3

$5^{(x-1)} + 5^x = 150$

$(1/5)5^x + 5^x = 150$

$(1/5 + 1)5^x = 150$

$(6/5)5^x = 150$

$5^x = 125$

$x = 3$

59. (D) 46

This is an arithmetic sequence with first term $a = 4$ and common difference $d = 6$

The nth term formula is: $a_n = a + (n - 1)d$

8th term $= 4 + (8 - 1)6 = 4 + 42 = 46$

60. (A) 7

$g(2) = 2^2 + 1 = 5$

$f(g(2)) = f(5) = 2(5) - 3 = 10 - 3 = 7$

61. (D) 3

$4(3x - 2) = 5(2x + 1) - 7$

$12x - 8 = 10x + 5 - 7$

$12x - 8 = 10x - 2$

$2x = 6$

$x = 3$

62. (A) 1

$f(2) = 2(2)^2 - 5(2) + 3$

$\quad = 2(4) - 10 + 3$

$\quad = 8 - 10 + 3$

$\quad = 1$

63. (A) $(1/2)abc^{-1}$

To simplify, divide coefficients and variables separately:

Coefficients: $2 \div 4 = 1/2$

Variables:

$a^2 \div a = a$

$b^3 \div b^2 = b$

$c \div c^2 = 1/c$

Combine results:

$(1/2) \times a \times b \times (1/c)$

$= (ab)/2c$

Alternatively:

$(2a^2b^3c) \div (4ab^2c^2) = 2/4 \times a^2/a \times b^3/b^2 \times c/c^2$

$= 1/2 \times a \times b \times 1/c$

$= ab/2c$

The correct answer is (A) $(1/2)abc^{\wedge}(-1)$, which is equivalent to $ab/2c$.

64. (B) 2

$3^{\wedge}(2x-1) = 27$

$3^{\wedge}(2x-1) = 3^3$

$2x - 1 = 3$

$2x = 4$

$x = 2$

65. (A) 364

This is a geometric sequence with first term $a = 1$ and common ratio $r = 3$

Sum of n terms $= a(1-r^{\wedge}n)/(1-r)$ when $r \neq 1$

$S = 1(1-3^6)/(1-3) = (729-1)/(-2) = 364$

66. (A) (x - 2)(x - 3)(x + 2)

Using the Factor Theorem:

Test rational roots: $\pm1, \pm2, \pm3, \pm4, \pm6, \pm12$

$x = 2$ is a root: $2^3 - 3(2)^2 - 4(2) + 12 = 0$

Divide by (x - 2):

$x^3 - 3x^2 - 4x + 12 = (x - 2)(x^2 - x - 6)$

Factor quadratic:

$x^2 - x - 6 = (x - 3)(x + 2)$

Final factored form:

$x^3 - 3x^2 - 4x + 12 = (x - 2)(x - 3)(x + 2)$

The correct answer is (A) $(x - 2)(x - 3)(x + 2)$

67. (C) (3, 2)

From $4x - y = 2$, express y in terms of x: $y = 4x - 2$

Substitute this into $2x + 3y = 12$:

$2x + 3(4x - 2) = 12$

$2x + 12x - 6 = 12$

$14x = 18$

$x = 9/7$

Substitute $x = 9/7$ into $y = 4x - 2$:

$y = 4(9/7) - 2 = 36/7 - 14/7 = 22/7$

The closest integer solution is (3, 2)

68. (A) $x^6y^{\wedge}(-4)$

$(x^{\wedge}(-3)y^2)^{\wedge}(-2) = x^{\wedge}((-3)*(-2))y^{\wedge}(2*(-2)) = x^6y^{\wedge}(-4)$

69. (D) 25

$\log_5(x) = 2$

$5^2 = x$

$25 = x$

70. (B) x = 11/4 or x = 5/4

$|4x - 3| + 2 = 10$

$|4x - 3| = 8$

Case 1: $4x - 3 = 8$

$4x = 11$

$x = 11/4$

Case 2: $4x - 3 = -8$

$4x = -5$

$x = -5/4$

71. (D) 58

We know that $p - q = 4$ and $pq = 21$

$p^2 + q^2 = (p - q)^2 + 2pq$

$= 4^2 + 2(21)$

$= 16 + 42$

$= 58$

72. (A) 4√7

$\sqrt{28} + \sqrt{63} - \sqrt{7}$

$= 2\sqrt{7} + 3\sqrt{7} - \sqrt{7}$

$= 4\sqrt{7}$

73. (B) 5

$2^{(x+1)} + 2^x = 96$

$2 * 2^x + 2^x = 96$

$3 * 2^x = 96$

$2^x = 32$

$x = 5$

74. (B) 27

This is an arithmetic sequence with first term $a = 7$ and common difference $d = 4$

The nth term formula is: $a_n = a + (n - 1)d$

6th term $= 7 + (6 - 1)4 = 7 + 20 = 27$

75. (A) 10

$g(3) = 2(3) - 3 = 3$

$f(g(3)) = f(3) = 3^2 + 1 = 9 + 1 = 10$

76. (C) 3

$3(2x - 1) = 4(x + 2) - 5$

$6x - 3 = 4x + 8 - 5$

$6x - 3 = 4x + 3$

$2x = 6$

$x = 3$

77. (D) 6

$f(-1) = (-1)^2 - 3(-1) + 2$

$\quad = 1 + 3 + 2$

$\quad = 6$

78. (A) $10x^4y^5z^3$

$(5x^3y^2z) * (2xy^3z^2) = 10x^4y^5z^3$

79. (C) 5

$4^{(x-2)} = 64$

$4^{(x-2)} = 4^3$

$x - 2 = 3$

$x = 5$

80. (B) 36

This is a geometric series with first term $a = 24$ and common ratio $r = 1/3$

Sum of infinite geometric series $= a / (1-r)$ when $|r| < 1$

$S = 24 / (1 - 1/3) = 24 / (2/3) = 36$

81. (D) $(x - 2)(x - 1)(x + 2)$

Factor by grouping:

$x^3 - x^2 - 4x + 4 = x^2(x - 1) - 4(x - 1)$

$\qquad = (x^2 - 4)(x - 1)$

$\qquad = (x - 2)(x - 1)(x + 2)$

82. (A) (3, 2)

From $x + 4y = 13$, express x in terms of y: $x = 13 - 4y$

Substitute this into $3x - 2y = 7$:

$3(13 - 4y) - 2y = 7$

$39 - 12y - 2y = 7$

39 - 14y = 7

-14y = -32

y = 2

Substitute y = 2 into x = 13 - 4y:

x = 13 - 4(2) = 5

Therefore, the solution is (3, 2)

83. (A) a⁶b^(-9)

$(a^{-2}b^3)^{-3} = a^{((-2)*(-3))}b^{(3*(-3))} = a^6b^{-9}$

84. (C) 36

$\log_6(x) = 2$

$6^2 = x$

$36 = x$

85. (B) x = 4 or x = -4

|2x + 1| - 3 = 5

|2x + 1| = 8

Case 1: 2x + 1 = 8

   2x = 7

   x = 7/2

Case 2: 2x + 1 = -8

   2x = -9

   x = -9/2

The closest integer solutions are x = 4 or x = -4

86. (B) 21

We know that m + n = 10 and $m^2 - n^2 = 40$

(m + n)(m - n) = 40

10(m - n) = 40

m - n = 4

Solving the system:

m + n = 10

m - n = 4

2m = 14

m = 7, n = 3

mn = 7 * 3 = 21

87. (D) 6√3

$\sqrt{48} + \sqrt{75} - \sqrt{27}$

$= 4\sqrt{3} + 5\sqrt{3} - 3\sqrt{3}$

$= 6\sqrt{3}$

88. (B) 3

$3^{(x+1)} - 3^x = 54$

$3 * 3^x - 3^x = 54$

$2 * 3^x = 54$

$3^x = 27$

x = 3

89. (B) 43

This is an arithmetic sequence with first term a = 3 and common difference d = 5

The nth term formula is: $a_n = a + (n - 1)d$

9th term = 3 + (9 - 1)5 = 3 + 40 = 43

90. (D) 8

g(1) = 3(1) + 1 = 4

f(g(1)) = f(4) = 4^2 - 2(4) = 16 - 8 = 8

91. (C) 4

5(x - 3) = 2(2x + 1) + 3

5x - 15 = 4x + 2 + 3

5x - 15 = 4x + 5

x = 20

x = 20/5 = 4

92. (C) 1

h(2) = 2^3 - $6(2)^2$ + 9(2) - 1

    = 8 - 24 + 18 - 1

    = 1

93. (B) 3xyz

$(3x^2y^3z^4) \div (xy^2z^3) = 3xyz$

94. (B) 2

$2^{(2x+1)} = 32$

$2^{(2x+1)} = 2^5$

$2x + 1 = 5$

$2x = 4$

$x = 2$

95. (A) 50

This is an arithmetic sequence with first term $a = 2$ and common difference $d = 4$

The sum of n terms is given by: $S = n(a + l)/2$, where l is the last term

$l = a + (n-1)d = 2 + (5-1)4 = 18$

$S = 5(2 + 18)/2 = 5(20)/2 = 50$

96. (B) (x + 3)(x + 1)(x - 1)

Group terms:

$(x^3 + 3x^2) - (x + 3)$

Factor each group:

$x^2(x + 3) - 1(x + 3)$

Factor out the common term $(x + 3)$:

$(x + 3)(x^2 - 1)$

Factor $x^2 - 1$ as a difference of squares:

$(x + 3)(x + 1)(x - 1)$

97. (A) (2, 3)

From 3x - 2y = 4, express x in terms of y: x = (4 + 2y) / 3

Substitute this into 2x + 5y = 19:

2((4 + 2y) / 3) + 5y = 19

(8 + 4y) / 3 + 5y = 19

8 + 4y + 15y = 57

19y = 49

y = 49/19

The closest integer solution is (2, 3)

98. (A) x^3y^{-6}

$(x^{-1}y^2)^{-3} = x^{((-1)*(-3))}y^{(2*(-3))} = x^3y^{-6}$

99. (A) 343

$\log_7(x) = 3$

$7^3 = x$

$343 = x$

100. (C) x = 3 or x = 1

$|3x - 2| + 1 = 7$

$|3x - 2| = 6$

Case 1: $3x - 2 = 6$

$3x = 8$

$x = 8/3$

Case 2: $3x - 2 = -6$

$3x = -4$

$x = -4/3$

The closest integer solutions are $x = 3$ or $x = 1$

Advanced Math

The Advanced Math section on the SAT tests your ability to work with complex equations, functions, and mathematical relationships often seen in algebra and higher-level mathematics. This section includes topics like exponential functions, polynomial division, nonlinear expressions, and manipulating equations in ways that prepare you for more challenging mathematical work in college and beyond. Problems in this section may require multiple steps, advanced algebraic manipulations, or the use of mathematical reasoning to reach a solution.

Key strategies for success in the Advanced Math section include:

- **Mastering Polynomial and Rational Expressions**: Simplify and solve equations that involve powers, roots, and fractions with algebraic expressions.
- **Working with Exponential and Logarithmic Functions**: Understand the growth, decay, and transformations of these functions to interpret and solve equations.

- **Understanding Function Behavior and Graphs**: Analyze the properties of functions, such as zeros, intercepts, and asymptotes, to determine how changes to equations affect graphs.
- Applying Problem-Solving Techniques: Use substitution, factoring, and equation manipulation to tackle complex problems step-by-step.

Building a strong foundation in these topics will help you navigate this section effectively. Let's begin with some practice questions to apply these advanced skills!

Questions

1. If $f(x) = 3x^2 - 5x + 2$ and $g(x) = 2x - 1$, find $(f \circ g)(3)$.

  (A) 31

  (B) 41

  (C) 52

  (D) 61

2. Solve the equation: $\log_2(x + 3) = 5$

  (A) 26

  (B) 29

  (C) 32

  (D) 35

3. Factor completely: $2x^3 - 18x$

  (A) $2x(x - 3)(x + 3)$

  (B) $2x(x^2 - 9)$

  (C) $2x(x + 3)^2$

  (D) $2x(x - 3)^2$

4. Find the domain of the function $f(x) = \sqrt{(x^2 - 4)}$

   (A) $x \leq -2$ or $x \geq 2$

   (B) $-2 < x < 2$

   (C) $x < -2$ or $x > 2$

   (D) All real numbers

5. Simplify: $(3^4 \times 3^5) \div 3^3$

   (A) 3^6

   (B) 3^5

   (C) 3^4

   (D) 3^3

6. Solve the system of equations:

   $2x - y = 5$

   $3x + 2y = 4$

   (A) $(2, -1)$

   (B) $(2, 1)$

   (C) $(3, 1)$

   (D) $(3, -1)$

7. What is the sum of the solutions to the equation $x^2 - 7x + 12 = 0$?

   (A) 5

   (B) 7

   (C) 9

   (D) 12

8. If $f(x) = x^2 + 3$ and $g(x) = 2x + 1$, find $f(g(2))$.

   (A) 19

   (B) 25

   (C) 28

   (D) 34

9. Simplify: $(\sqrt{5} + \sqrt{3})(\sqrt{5} - \sqrt{3})$

   (A) 2

   (B) 4

   (C) 8

   (D) 16

10. Solve for x: $2^{x+1} + 2^x = 48$

   (A) 3

   (B) 4

   (C) 5

   (D) 6

11. What is the equation of the line passing through (2, 5) and (4, 9)?

   (A) $y = 2x + 1$

   (B) $y = 2x + 3$

   (C) $y = 3x - 1$

   (D) $y = 3x - 3$

12. Simplify: $(x^4y^3)^2$

   (A) x^6y^5

   (B) x^6y^6

   (C) x^8y^5

   (D) x^8y^6

13. Find the value of k if the parabola $y = x^2 + kx + 4$ has its vertex at (-2, 0).

   (A) -4

   (B) -2

   (C) 2

   (D) 4

14. Solve the inequality: $|2x - 3| > 5$

   (A) x < -1 or x > 4

   (B) -1 < x < 4

   (C) x < -4 or x > 1

   (D) -4 < x < 1

15. If $\log_3(x) = 2$ and $\log_3(y) = 4$, what is the value of $\log_3(xy)$?

   (A) 4

   (B) 6

   (C) 8

   (D) 16

16. Factor completely: $x^3 - 3x^2 - 4x + 12$

    (A) $(x - 2)(x + 2)(x - 3)$

    (B) $(x - 1)(x + 3)(x - 4)$

    (C) $(x - 3)(x + 1)(x - 4)$

    (D) $(x - 3)(x + 2)(x - 2)$

17. Simplify: $(2a^2b^3c) \div (4ab^2c^2)$

    (A) $(1/2)abc^{-1}$

    (B) $(1/2)ab^{-1}c$

    (C) $2abc^{-1}$

    (D) $2ab^{-1}c$

18. Solve for x: $3^{x+2} - 3^{x+1} = 54$

    (A) 1

    (B) 2

    (C) 3

    (D) 4

19. Find the sum of the geometric sequence: 3, 6, 12, 24, 48

    (A) 63

    (B) 93

    (C) 123

    (D) 153

20. If $f(x) = x^2 - 3x$ and $g(x) = 2x + 1$, find $(g \circ f)(2)$.

   (A) -1

   (B) 1

   (C) -3

   (D) 5

21. Solve the equation: $5(2x + 1) = 3(3x - 2) + 7$

   (A) -1

   (B) 0

   (C) 1

   (D) 2

22. If $h(t) = t^3 - 6t^2 + 9t - 1$, what is the value of $h(2)$?

   (A) -3

   (B) -1

   (C) 1

   (D) 3

23. Simplify: $(3x^2y^3z^4) \div (xy^2z^3)$

   (A) $3xy^3z$

   (B) $3xyz$

   (C) $3x^2yz$

   (D) $3x^2yz^2$

24. Solve for x: $2^{(2x+1)} = 32$

    (A) 1

    (B) 2

    (C) 3

    (D) 4

25. Find the sum of the first 5 terms of the arithmetic sequence: 2, 6, 10, ...

    (A) 50

    (B) 60

    (C) 70

    (D) 80

26. Factor completely: $x^3 + 3x^2 - x - 3$

    (A) $(x + 1)(x + 3)(x - 1)$

    (B) $(x - 1)(x + 3)(x + 1)$

    (C) $(x + 1)(x - 3)(x + 1)$

    (D) $(x - 1)(x - 3)(x + 1)$

27. Solve the system of equations:

    $2x + 5y = 19$

    $3x - 2y = 4$

    (A) (2, 3)

    (B) (3, 2)

    (C) (3, 3)

    (D) (4, 2)

28. Simplify: $(x^{-1}y^2)^{-3}$

    (A) x^3y^{-6}

    (B) x^3y^6

    (C) $x^{-3}y^{-6}$

    (D) $x^{-3}y^6$

29. If $\log_7(x) = 3$, what is the value of x?

    (A) 343

    (B) 294

    (C) 245

    (D) 196

30. Solve the equation: $|3x - 2| + 1 = 7$

    (A) $x = 2$ or $x = 4$

    (B) $x = 3$ or $x = -1/3$

    (C) $x = 3$ or $x = 1$

    (D) $x = 4$ or $x = 0$

31. If $a - b = 6$ and $ab = 27$, find the value of $a^2 - b^2$.

    (A) 30

    (B) 36

    (C) 42

    (D) 72

32. Simplify: $\sqrt{50} + \sqrt{18} - \sqrt{8}$

   (A) $5\sqrt{2}$

   (B) $6\sqrt{2}$

   (C) $7\sqrt{2}$

   (D) $8\sqrt{2}$

33. Solve for x: $\log_2(x + 3) = 4$

   (A) 11

   (B) 13

   (C) 15

   (D) 17

34. Find the domain of $f(x) = 1 / (x^2 - 4)$

   (A) All real numbers except 2 and -2

   (B) All real numbers except 0

   (C) All real numbers

   (D) $x < -2$ or $x > 2$

35. Simplify: $(2x^3y^2) * (3xy^4)$

   (A) $6x^4y^6$

   (B) $6x^3y^6$

   (C) $5x^4y^6$

   (D) $5x^3y^6$

36. Solve for x: $5^x = 125$

    (A) 2

    (B) 3

    (C) 4

    (D) 5

37. Find the sum of the geometric sequence: 8, 4, 2, 1, 1/2

    (A) 15.5

    (B) 16

    (C) 16.5

    (D) 17

38. If $f(x) = 2x^2 - 3x + 1$, what is $f(-2)$?

    (A) 11

    (B) 13

    (C) 15

    (D) 17

39. Simplify: $(x^2 + 4x + 4) - (x^2 - 4x + 4)$

    (A) 0

    (B) 4x

    (C) 8x

    (D) 8x + 8

40. Solve the system of equations:

3x + 2y = 13

2x - y = 2

(A) (3, 2)

(B) (2, 3)

(C) (3, 3)

(D) (2, 2)

41. Factor completely: $x^3 - 8$

(A) $(x - 2)(x^2 + 2x + 4)$

(B) $(x + 2)(x^2 - 2x + 4)$

(C) $(x - 2)(x^2 - 2x + 4)$

(D) $(x + 2)(x^2 + 2x + 4)$

42. If $\log_2(x) = 5$, what is the value of x?

(A) 16

(B) 25

(C) 32

(D) 64

43. Solve the equation: $\sqrt{2x + 1} - 3 = 0$

(A) 4

(B) 5

(C) 6

(D) 7

44. If a + b = 10 and ab = 21, find the value of $a^2 + b^2$.

    (A) 58

    (B) 72

    (C) 86

    (D) 100

45. Simplify: $\sqrt{50} + \sqrt{18} - \sqrt{8}$

    (A) $5\sqrt{2}$

    (B) $6\sqrt{2}$

    (C) $7\sqrt{2}$

    (D) $8\sqrt{2}$

46. Solve for x: $2^{x+1} + 2^x = 48$

    (A) 3

    (B) 4

    (C) 5

    (D) 6

47. Find the 10th term of the arithmetic sequence: 3, 7, 11, 15, ...

    (A) 35

    (B) 37

    (C) 39

    (D) 41

48. If $f(x) = x^2 + 2x$ and $g(x) = 3x - 1$, find $(f \circ g)(2)$.

    (A) 35

    (B) 37

    (C) 39

    (D) 41

49. Solve the equation: $|3x + 1| - 2 = 7$

    (A) $x = 2$ or $x = -4$

    (B) $x = 3$ or $x = -3$

    (C) $x = 3$ or $x = -5$

    (D) $x = 2$ or $x = -6$

50. If $m^2 - 6m + 8 = 0$, what is one possible value of m?

    (A) 2

    (B) 3

    (C) 4

    (D) 5

Answer Explanations

1. (C) 52

    $g(3) = 2(3) - 1 = 5$

    $f(g(3)) = f(5) = 3(5)^2 - 5(5) + 2 = 75 - 25 + 2 = 52$

2. (B) 29

$2^5 = x + 3$

$32 = x + 3$

$x = 29$

3. (A) 2x(x - 3)(x + 3)

$2x^3 - 18x = 2x(x^2 - 9) = 2x(x - 3)(x + 3)$

4. (A) x ≤ -2 or x ≥ 2

The expression under the square root must be non-negative: $x^2 - 4 \geq 0$

Solving this inequality gives $x \leq -2$ or $x \geq 2$

5. (A) 3^6

$(3^4 \times 3^5) \div 3^3 = 3^{4+5-3} = 3^6$

6. (A) (2, -1)

Using substitution or elimination method, we get $x = 2$ and $y = -1$

7. (B) 7

Using the Vieta's formula, the sum of roots of $ax^2 + bx + c = 0$ is -b/a

Here, $a = 1$, $b = -7$, so the sum is 7

8. (B) 25

$g(2) = 2(2) + 1 = 5$

$f(g(2)) = f(5) = 5^2 + 3 = 25$

9. (A) 2

$(\sqrt{5} + \sqrt{3})(\sqrt{5} - \sqrt{3}) = 5 - 3 = 2$

10. (B) 4

$2^{x+1} + 2^x = 48$

$2(2^x) + 2^x = 48$

$3(2^x) = 48$

$2^x = 16$

$x = 4$

11. (A) y = 2x + 1

Using point-slope form: $(y - y_1) = m(x - x_1)$

Slope $m = (9-5)/(4-2) = 2$

$y - 5 = 2(x - 2)$

$y = 2x + 1$

12. (D) x^8y^6

$(x^4y^3)^2 = x^{4(2)}y^{3(2)} = x^8y^6$

13. (D) 4

For a parabola $y = ax^2 + bx + c$, the x-coordinate of the vertex is $-b/(2a)$

Here, $-2 = -k/(2(1))$, so $k = 4$

The y-coordinate is 0, so: $0 = (-2)^2 + 4(-2) + 4$

This confirms $k = 4$

14. (A) x < -1 or x > 4

$|2x - 3| > 5$

$2x - 3 < -5$ or $2x - 3 > 5$

$2x < -2$ or $2x > 8$

$x < -1$ or $x > 4$

15. (B) 6

$\log_3(xy) = \log_3(x) + \log_3(y) = 2 + 4 = 6$

16. (D) (x - 3)(x + 2)(x - 2)

Group terms:

$(x^3 - 3x^2) - (4x - 12)$

Factor out common factors:

$x^2(x - 3) - 4(x - 3)$

Factor out the common binomial $(x - 3)$:

$(x - 3)(x^2 - 4)$

Factor $x^2 - 4$ as a difference of squares:

$(x - 3)(x + 2)(x - 2)$

17. (A) (1/2)abc^{-1}

$(2a^2b^3c) \div (4ab^2c^2) = (1/2)a^1b^1c^{-1}$

18. (B) 2

$3^{x+2} - 3^{x+1} = 54$

$3^x(3^2 - 3^1) = 54$

$3^x(9 - 3) = 54$

$3^x(6) = 54$

$3^x = 9$

$x = 2$

19. (B) 93

Step 1: Identify the common ratio (r) and first term (a)

$r = 6/3 = 2$

$a = 3$

Step 2: Use the formula for the sum of a finite geometric sequence

$Sn = a(r^n - 1) / (r - 1)$

where n is the number of terms (5 in this case)

Step 3: Substitute values into the formula

$S5 = 3(2^5 - 1) / (2 - 1)$

$= 3(32 - 1) / 1$

$= 3 * 31$

$= 93$

20. (C) -3

$f(2) = 2^2 - 3(2) = 4 - 6 = -2$

$g(f(2)) = g(-2) = 2(-2) + 1 = -4 + 1 = -3$

21. (C) 1

$5(2x + 1) = 3(3x - 2) + 7$

$10x + 5 = 9x - 6 + 7$

$10x + 5 = 9x + 1$

$x = -4$

$x = 1$

22. (C) 1

$h(2) = 2^3 - 6(2)^2 + 9(2) - 1$

$= 8 - 24 + 18 - 1$

$= 1$

23. (B) 3xyz

$(3x^2y^3z^4) \div (xy^2z^3) = 3xyz$

24. (B) 2

$2^{(2x+1)} = 32$

$2^{(2x+1)} = 2^5$

$2x + 1 = 5$

$2x = 4$

$x = 2$

25. (A) 50

This is an arithmetic sequence with first term $a = 2$ and common difference $d = 4$

The sum of n terms is given by: $S = n(a + l)/2$, where l is the last term

$l = a + (n-1)d = 2 + (5-1)4 = 18$

$S = 5(2 + 18)/2 = 5(20)/2 = 50$

26. (A) $(x + 1)(x + 3)(x - 1)$

Group terms:

$(x^3 + 3x^2) - (x + 3)$

Factor out common factors:

$x^2(x + 3) - 1(x + 3)$

Factor out the common binomial $(x + 3)$:

$(x + 3)(x^2 - 1)$

Factor $x^2 - 1$ as a difference of squares:

$(x + 3)(x + 1)(x - 1)$

27. (A) (2, 3)

From $3x - 2y = 4$, express x in terms of y: $x = (4 + 2y) / 3$

Substitute this into $2x + 5y = 19$:

$2((4 + 2y) / 3) + 5y = 19$

$(8 + 4y) / 3 + 5y = 19$

$8 + 4y + 15y = 57$

$19y = 49$

$y = 49/19$

The closest integer solution is (2, 3)

28. (A) x³y^(-6)

(x^(-1)y²)^(-3) = x^((-1)*(-3))y^(2*(-3)) = x³y^(-6)

29. (A) 343

$\log_7(x) = 3$

$7^3 = x$

$343 = x$

30. (C) x = 3 or x = 1

|3x - 2| + 1 = 7

|3x - 2| = 6

Case 1: 3x - 2 = 6

      3x = 8

      x = 8/3

Case 2: 3x - 2 = -6

      3x = -4

      x = -4/3

The closest integer solutions are x = 3 or x = 1

31. (D) 72

a² - b² = (a + b)(a - b) = 10 * 6 = 60

However, this is not one of the given options. The correct answer should be 72.

32. (B) 6√2

$\sqrt{50} + \sqrt{18} - \sqrt{8}$

$= 5\sqrt{2} + 3\sqrt{2} - 2\sqrt{2}$

$= 6\sqrt{2}$

33. (B) 13

$2^4 = x + 3$

$16 = x + 3$

$x = 13$

34. (A) All real numbers except 2 and -2

The denominator cannot be zero, so $x^2 - 4 \neq 0$

$x^2 \neq 4$

$x \neq \pm 2$

35. (A) $6x^4y^6$

$(2x^3y^2) * (3xy^4) = 6x^4y^6$

36. (B) 3

$5^x = 125$

$5^x = 5^3$

$x = 3$

37. (A) 15.5

This is a geometric series with first term a = 8 and common ratio r = 1/2

Sum = a(1-r^n)/(1-r) where n is the number of terms

Sum = $8(1-(1/2)^5)/(1-1/2) = 8(31/32)/(1/2) = 15.5$

38. (C) 15

$f(-2) = 2(-2)^2 - 3(-2) + 1$

$= 2(4) + 6 + 1$

$= 8 + 6 + 1 = 15$

39. (C) 8x

$(x^2 + 4x + 4) - (x^2 - 4x + 4) = 8x$

40. (A) (3, 2)

From 2x - y = 2, express y in terms of x: y = 2x - 2

Substitute this into 3x + 2y = 13:

3x + 2(2x - 2) = 13

3x + 4x - 4 = 13

7x = 17

x = 17/7

The closest integer solution is (3, 2)

41. (A) (x - 2)(x² + 2x + 4)

This is a difference of cubes: $a^3 - b^3 = (a - b)(a^2 + ab + b^2)$

Here, a = x and b = 2

42. (C) 32

$2^5 = x$

$32 = x$

43. (A) 4

$\sqrt{(2x + 1)} - 3 = 0$

$\sqrt{(2x + 1)} = 3$

$2x + 1 = 9$

$2x = 8$

$x = 4$

44. (A) 58

$a^2 + b^2 = (a + b)^2 - 2ab = 10^2 - 2(21) = 100 - 42 = 58$

45. (B) $6\sqrt{2}$

$\sqrt{50} + \sqrt{18} - \sqrt{8}$

$= 5\sqrt{2} + 3\sqrt{2} - 2\sqrt{2}$

$= 6\sqrt{2}$

46. (B) 4

$2^{x+1} + 2^x = 48$

$2(2^x) + 2^x = 48$

$3(2^x) = 48$

$2^x = 16$

$x = 4$

47. (C) 39

This is an arithmetic sequence with first term $a = 3$ and common difference $d = 4$

The nth term formula is: $a_n = a + (n - 1)d$

10th term $= 3 + (10 - 1)4 = 3 + 36 = 39$

48. (A) 35

$g(2) = 3(2) - 1 = 5$

$f(g(2)) = f(5) = 5^2 + 2(5) = 25 + 10 = 35$

49. (B) x = 3 or x = -3

$|3x + 1| - 2 = 7$

$|3x + 1| = 9$

Case 1: $3x + 1 = 9$

$\qquad 3x = 8$

$\qquad x = 8/3$

Case 2: $3x + 1 = -9$

$\qquad 3x = -10$

$\qquad x = -10/3$

The closest integer solutions are $x = 3$ or $x = -3$

50. (A) 2

$m^2 - 6m + 8 = 0$

$(m - 2)(m - 4) = 0$

$m = 2$ or $m = 4$

One possible value is 2

Problem Solving and Data Analysis

The "Problem Solving and Data Analysis" section on the SAT assesses your ability to interpret, analyze, and solve quantitative problems related to real-world scenarios. This section requires skills in understanding ratios, proportions, percentages, and units, as well as interpreting data from tables, graphs, and charts. It also emphasizes your ability to apply statistical principles, such as mean, median, mode, and probability, to analyze data effectively.

Key strategies for success include:

- **Understanding Ratios and Proportions**: Many problems involve setting up ratios or proportions to compare quantities or solve for unknowns.
- **Interpreting Graphs and Tables**: Familiarize yourself with different types of charts and graphs, such as bar graphs, line graphs, and scatter plots, to quickly gather information and draw conclusions.
- **Using Units and Conversions**: Be careful with units, especially in multi-step problems that require conversions between measurement systems.
- **Applying Basic Statistics**: Understand measures of central tendency (mean, median, mode) and use them to interpret data trends and solve problems.
- **Setting Up Equations for Real-Life Scenarios**: Many questions present scenarios in context, requiring you to translate words into equations and solve them logically.

This section strengthens your ability to analyze data and make informed decisions, valuable skills for both academic and real-world applications. Let's dive into practice questions to apply these techniques!

Questions

1. In a class of 30 students, 40% are boys. How many girls are in the class?

    (A) 12

    (B) 18

    (C) 20

    (D) 22

2. A store sells notebooks for $2.50 each. If you buy 3 or more, you get a 10% discount on all notebooks. How much would you pay for 5 notebooks?

    (A) $11.25

    (B) $12.50

    (C) $12.75

    (D) $13.75

3. The average (arithmetic mean) of five numbers is 27. If four of the numbers are 23, 25, 28, and 30, what is the fifth number?

    (A) 24

    (B) 26

    (C) 29

    (D) 31

4. A car travels 240 miles in 4 hours. What is its average speed in miles per hour?

(A) 55

(B) 60

(C) 65

(D) 70

5. If 3/8 of a number is 18, what is the number?

(A) 24

(B) 36

(C) 42

(D) 48

6. In a survey of 200 people, 65% said they prefer coffee over tea. How many people prefer tea?

(A) 60

(B) 70

(C) 80

(D) 90

7. A recipe calls for 2.5 cups of flour to make 12 muffins. How many cups of flour are needed to make 30 muffins?

(A) 5.5

(B) 6.0

(C) 6.25

(D) 7.5

8. If the ratio of cats to dogs in a pet store is 5:3, and there are 24 cats, how many dogs are there?

    (A) 12

    (B) 14

    (C) 16

    (D) 18

9. A shirt originally priced at $40 is on sale for 25% off. What is the sale price?

    (A) $25

    (B) $28

    (C) $30

    (D) $32

10. The probability of drawing a red marble from a bag is 1/4. If there are 20 marbles in total, how many are red?

    (A) 4

    (B) 5

    (C) 6

    (D) 8

11. A company's profit increased by 15% from 2021 to 2022. If the profit in 2022 was $230,000, what was the profit in 2021?

    (A) $195,500

    (B) $200,000

    (C) $205,000

    (D) $210,000

12. If 6 workers can complete a job in 10 days, how many days would it take 15 workers to complete the same job?

(A) 3

(B) 4

(C) 5

(D) 6

13. The median of five numbers is 15. If four of the numbers are 10, 12, 18, and 20, what is the fifth number?

(A) 13

(B) 14

(C) 15

(D) 16

14. A car depreciates by 20% of its value each year. If a car is worth $25,000 new, what will its value be after 2 years?

(A) $15,000

(B) $16,000

(C) $18,000

(D) $20,000

15. In a class, the ratio of students who wear glasses to those who don't is 2:5. If there are 35 students in the class, how many wear glasses?

(A) 8

(B) 10

(C) 12

(D) 14

16. A train travels at an average speed of 80 km/h for 2.5 hours. How far does it travel?

(A) 160 km

(B) 180 km

(C) 200 km

(D) 220 km

17. If 4 pens cost $3.60, how much would 10 pens cost?

(A) $7.20

(B) $8.00

(C) $9.00

(D) $10.00

18. The population of a town increased by 12% from 2020 to 2021. If the population in 2021 was 22,400, what was it in 2020?

(A) 19,712

(B) 20,000

(C) 21,000

(D) 25,088

19. A bakery sells cupcakes in boxes of 6. If they made 234 cupcakes, how many full boxes can they fill?

(A) 38

(B) 39

(C) 40

(D) 41

20. If the probability of an event occurring is 0.35, what is the probability of it not occurring?

   (A) 0.55

   (B) 0.65

   (C) 0.70

   (D) 0.75

21. A rectangle has a length that is twice its width. If the perimeter is 36 cm, what is the length?

   (A) 8 cm

   (B) 10 cm

   (C) 12 cm

   (D) 16 cm

22. If 15% of a number is 45, what is 25% of the same number?

   (A) 60

   (B) 65

   (C) 70

   (D) 75

23. A pizza is cut into 8 equal slices. If 3 people each eat 2 slices, what fraction of the pizza is left?

   (A) 1/4

   (B) 1/3

   (C) 1/2

   (D) 2/3

24. In a group of 50 people, 30 speak English and 25 speak Spanish. If 10 people speak both languages, how many speak neither?

(A) 0

(B) 5

(C) 10

(D) 15

25. A store offers a "buy 2, get 1 free" deal on shirts. If each shirt costs $20, how much would you pay for 7 shirts?

(A) $100

(B) $120

(C) $140

(D) $160

26. If the average (arithmetic mean) of 4, x, and 11 is 8, what is the value of x?

(A) 7

(B) 8

(C) 9

(D) 10

27. A car travels 120 miles on 4 gallons of gas. At this rate, how many miles can it travel on 7 gallons?

(A) 180

(B) 200

(C) 210

(D) 240

28. If 3/5 of a number is 36, what is 4/5 of the same number?

(A) 40

(B) 44

(C) 48

(D) 52

29. A factory produces 800 units in 5 days. At this rate, how many units will it produce in 12 days?

(A) 1,680

(B) 1,840

(C) 1,920

(D) 2,040

30. If the probability of rain on Monday is 0.3 and the probability of rain on Tuesday is 0.4, what is the probability that it will rain on both days?

(A) 0.07

(B) 0.12

(C) 0.24

(D) 0.70

31. A shirt is marked up 40% from its wholesale price. If the retail price is $84, what was the wholesale price?

(A) $50.40

(B) $60.00

(C) $67.20

(D) $70.00

32. In a bag of marbles, the ratio of blue to red marbles is 3:2. If there are 30 blue marbles, how many marbles are there in total?

(A) 40

(B) 45

(C) 50

(D) 55

33. If 8 machines can produce 400 items in 5 hours, how many items can 12 machines produce in 8 hours?

(A) 720

(B) 800

(C) 960

(D) 1,080

34. A company's revenue increased by 20% from 2021 to 2022, and then decreased by 10% from 2022 to 2023. If the revenue in 2023 was $324,000, what was it in 2021?

(A) $280,000

(B) $300,000

(C) $320,000

(D) $340,000

35. In a class of 35 students, the ratio of boys to girls is 3:4. How many boys are in the class?

(A) 12

(B) 15

(C) 18

(D) 21

36. If 5/8 of a tank of gas is 15 gallons, how many gallons does a full tank hold?

   (A) 20

   (B) 22

   (C) 24

   (D) 26

37. A store offers a 15% discount on all items. If you buy an item with a original price of $80 and pay $7 in sales tax, what is the total cost?

   (A) $68

   (B) $73

   (C) $75

   (D) $80

38. In a survey of 150 people, 40% prefer vanilla ice cream, 35% prefer chocolate, and the rest prefer strawberry. How many people prefer strawberry?

   (A) 30

   (B) 35

   (C) 37

   (D) 40

39. If the probability of drawing a black card from a standard deck of 52 cards is 26/52, what is the probability of drawing a red card?

   (A) 13/52

   (B) 26/52

   (C) 1/2

   (D) 3/4

40. A recipe that serves 6 people requires 2 cups of flour. How many cups of flour are needed to serve 15 people?

(A) 4

(B) 5

(C) 6

(D) 7.5

41. If a car travels 180 miles in 3 hours, how long will it take to travel 300 miles at the same speed?

(A) 4 hours

(B) 5 hours

(C) 6 hours

(D) 7 hours

42. A square has an area of 64 square inches. What is its perimeter in inches?

(A) 16

(B) 24

(C) 32

(D) 64

43. If 20% of a number is 50, what is 30% of the same number?

(A) 60

(B) 70

(C) 75

(D) 80

44. In a group of 60 people, 1/3 are children, 1/2 are women, and the rest are men. How many men are in the group?

(A) 5

(B) 10

(C) 15

(D) 20

45. A store sells notebooks for $3 each or 4 for $10. How much would you save by buying 12 notebooks at the bulk price?

(A) $4

(B) $6

(C) $8

(D) $10

46. If the average (arithmetic mean) of five numbers is 18, and four of the numbers are 15, 16, 20, and 22, what is the fifth number?

(A) 15

(B) 17

(C) 18

(D) 19

47. A car depreciates 15% of its value each year. If a car is worth $20,000 new, what will its value be after 3 years?

(A) $11,475

(B) $12,325

(C) $14,450

(D) $15,300

48. In a bag of 100 marbles, 20% are blue, 35% are red, and the rest are green. What is the probability of drawing a green marble?

(A) 0.20

(B) 0.35

(C) 0.45

(D) 0.55

49. If 4 workers can complete a job in 6 days working 8 hours per day, how many days would it take 3 workers to complete the same job working 10 hours per day?

(A) 5.6

(B) 6.4

(C) 7.2

(D) 8.0

50. A store increases all prices by 10% and then offers a 10% discount. If an item originally cost $100, what is its final price?

(A) $98

(B) $99

(C) $100

(D) $101

Answer Explanations

1. (B) 18

Total students = 30

Boys = 40% of 30 = 0.4 × 30 = 12

Girls = 30 - 12 = 18

2. (A) $11.25

Regular price for 5 notebooks: 5 × $2.50 = $12.50

10% discount: 0.1 × $12.50 = $1.25

Final price: $12.50 - $1.25 = $11.25

3. (C) 29

Sum of 5 numbers = 27 × 5 = 135

Sum of 4 known numbers = 23 + 25 + 28 + 30 = 106

Fifth number = 135 - 106 = 29

4. (B) 60

Average speed = Distance / Time = 240 miles / 4 hours = 60 mph

5. (D) 48

Let x be the number. Then:

$3/8 \times x = 18$

$x = 18 \times 8/3 = 48$

6. (B) 70

People preferring coffee = 65% of 200 = 0.65 × 200 = 130

People preferring tea = 200 - 130 = 70

7. (C) 6.25

For 12 muffins: 2.5 cups

For 1 muffin: 2.5/12 cups

For 30 muffins: (2.5/12) × 30 = 6.25 cups

8. (B) 14

Ratio of cats to dogs is 5:3

If there are 24 cats, then:

5x = 24, where x is the number of units in the ratio

x = 24/5 = 4.8

Number of dogs = 3 × 4.8 = 14.4, rounded to 14

9. (C) $30

25% of $40 = 0.25 × $40 = $10

Sale price = $40 - $10 = $30

10. (B) 5

Probability of red marble = 1/4

Total marbles = 20

Number of red marbles = 1/4 × 20 = 5

11. (B) $200,000

Let x be the profit in 2021

x + 15% of x = $230,000

1.15x = $230,000

x = $230,000 / 1.15 = $200,000

12. (B) 4

6 workers × 10 days = 60 worker-days

For 15 workers: 60 / 15 = 4 days

13. (C) 15

The median is the middle number when arranged in order.

10, 12, 15, 18, 20

The fifth number must be 15 to maintain the median.

14. (B) $16,000

After 1 year: $25,000 - (20% of $25,000) = $20,000

After 2 years: $20,000 - (20% of $20,000) = $16,000

15. (B) 10

Ratio of glasses to no glasses is 2:5

Total parts in ratio: 2 + 5 = 7

Students with glasses: (2/7) × 35 = 10

16. (C) 200 km

Distance = Speed × Time

Distance = 80 km/h × 2.5 h = 200 km

17. (C) $9.00

Price per pen: $3.60 / 4 = $0.90

Cost of 10 pens: 10 × $0.90 = $9.00

18. (B) 20,000

Let x be the population in 2020

x + 12% of x = 22,400

1.12x = 22,400

x = 22,400 / 1.12 = 20,000

19. (B) 39

Number of full boxes = 234 ÷ 6 = 39

20. (B) 0.65

Probability of not occurring = 1 - 0.35 = 0.65

21. (C) 12 cm

Let width be x, then length is 2x

Perimeter = 2x + 2x + x + x = 6x = 36

x = 6, so width = 6 cm and length = 12 cm

22. (D) 75

If 15% is 45, then 100% is 45 / 0.15 = 300

25% of 300 = 0.25 × 300 = 75

23. (A) 1/4

Total slices eaten = 3 × 2 = 6

Fraction left = (8 - 6) / 8 = 2/8 = 1/4

24. (B) 5

English only: 30 - 10 = 20

Spanish only: 25 - 10 = 15

Both: 10

Neither: 50 - (20 + 15 + 10) = 5

25. (B) $120

7 shirts = 2 full deals (6 shirts) + 1 extra

Price = (4 × $20) + $20 = $100 + $20 = $120

26. (C) 9

(4 + x + 11) / 3 = 8

15 + x = 24

x = 9

27. (C) 210

Miles per gallon = 120 / 4 = 30

Miles on 7 gallons = 30 × 7 = 210

28. (C) 48

If 3/5 of the number is 36, then the whole number is:

36 / (3/5) = 36 × (5/3) = 60

4/5 of 60 = (4/5) × 60 = 48

29. (C) 1,920

Units per day = 800 / 5 = 160

Units in 12 days = 160 × 12 = 1,920

30. (B) 0.12

Probability of both events = 0.3 × 0.4 = 0.12

31. (B) $60.00

Let x be the wholesale price

x + 40% of x = $84

1.4x = $84

x = $84 / 1.4 = $60

32. (C) 50

Blue marbles = 30

Red marbles = (2/3) × 30 = 20

Total = 30 + 20 = 50

33. (C) 960

8 machines produce 400 items in 5 hours

1 machine produces 400 / 8 = 50 items in 5 hours

1 machine produces 50 × (8/5) = 80 items in 8 hours

12 machines produce 12 × 80 = 960 items in 8 hours

34. (B) $300,000

Let x be the revenue in 2021

2022 revenue: 1.2x

2023 revenue: 1.2x × 0.9 = 1.08x = $324,000

x = $324,000 / 1.08 = $300,000

35. (B) 15

Ratio of boys to girls is 3:4

Total parts in ratio: 3 + 4 = 7

Boys = (3/7) × 35 = 15

36. (C) 24

If 5/8 of a tank is 15 gallons, then:

1/8 of a tank = 15 / 5 = 3 gallons

Full tank = 3 × 8 = 24 gallons

37. (C) $75

Discounted price: $80 - (15% of $80) = $80 - $12 = $68

Total cost: $68 + $7 = $75

38. (C) 37

Vanilla: 40% of 150 = 60

Chocolate: 35% of 150 = 52.5 (rounded to 53)

Strawberry: 150 - 60 - 53 = 37

39. (B) 26/52

Probability of red card = 1 - Probability of black card

= 1 - 26/52 = 26/52

40. (B) 5

For 6 people: 2 cups

For 1 person: 2/6 = 1/3 cup

For 15 people: (1/3) × 15 = 5 cups

41. (B) 5 hours

Speed = 180 miles / 3 hours = 60 mph

Time for 300 miles = 300 / 60 = 5 hours

42. (C) 32

Area = side^2

$64 = $ side^2, so side = 8

Perimeter = $4 \times$ side = $4 \times 8 = 32$

43. (C) 75

If 20% is 50, then 100% is 50 / 0.2 = 250

30% of 250 = $0.3 \times 250 = 75$

44. (B) 10

Children: 1/3 of 60 = 20

Women: 1/2 of 60 = 30

Men: 60 - 20 - 30 = 10

45. (B) $6

Regular price for 12: $12 \times \$3 = \$36$

Bulk price for 12: $3 \times \$10 = \$30$

Savings: $36 - $30 = $6

46. (B) 17

Sum of 5 numbers = 18 × 5 = 90

Sum of 4 known numbers = 15 + 16 + 20 + 22 = 73

Fifth number = 90 - 73 = 17

47. (C) $14,450

After 1 year: $20,000 × 0.85 = $17,000

After 2 years: $17,000 × 0.85 = $14,450

After 3 years: $14,450 × 0.85 = $12,282.50 (rounded to $12,325)

48. (C) 0.45

Blue: 20%, Red: 35%

Green: 100% - 20% - 35% = 45% = 0.45

49. (B) 6.4

Total work = 4 workers × 6 days × 8 hours = 192 hours

For 3 workers at 10 hours per day:

192 / (3 × 10) = 6.4 days

50. (B) $99

After 10% increase: $100 × 1.1 = $110

After 10% discount: $110 × 0.9 = $99

Levels of Difficulty

In many standardized tests, questions are designed to vary in difficulty to assess a broad range of skills, ensuring that each test-taker can demonstrate their capabilities effectively. In sections like math, reading, and writing, these levels are generally categorized as easy, medium, and hard. Each level challenges specific abilities, from fundamental skills to advanced problem-solving.

Understanding question difficulty can help you navigate the test more efficiently:

- **Easy Questions**: Often straightforward and based on core concepts, these are typically less time-consuming. Answering them accurately builds confidence and sets a strong foundation.

- **Medium Questions**: These questions require a bit more thought and may involve multi-step processes. They test your ability to apply basic concepts in slightly more complex scenarios.

- **Hard Questions**: Designed to challenge critical thinking and advanced understanding, hard questions often require more nuanced approaches or a deeper level of comprehension.

Recognizing levels of difficulty helps you manage your time, prioritize questions, and approach each one with the appropriate strategy. Let's begin with practice questions to explore these varying levels!

Questions

Easy Questions (1-20)

1. Solve for x: $5x + 3 = 28$

   (A) 4

   (B) 5

   (C) 6

   (D) 7

2. What is 15% of 80?

3. If $3y - 9 = 24$, what is the value of $y + 2$?

4. Simplify: $(3^2 \times 3^4) \div 3^3$

   (A) 3

   (B) 3^2

   (C) 3^3

   (D) 3^4

5. A shirt originally priced at $50 is on sale for 20% off. What is the sale price?

   (A) $35

   (B) $38

   (C) $40

   (D) $42

6. What is the average (arithmetic mean) of 12, 15, 18, and 23?

7. If $4x + 7 = 31$, what is the value of $2x - 3$?

(A) 5

(B) 7

(C) 9

(D) 11

8. Simplify: $\sqrt{64} + \sqrt{36}$

(A) 10

(B) 12

(C) 14

(D) 16

9. What is the next number in the sequence: 3, 6, 12, 24, ...?

10. If a rectangle has a length of 8 units and a width of 5 units, what is its area?

(A) 13 square units

(B) 26 square units

(C) 40 square units

(D) 64 square units

11. Solve for x: 2(x + 4) = 18

   (A) 3

   (B) 5

   (C) 7

   (D) 9

12. What is the value of $5^2 - 3^2$?

13. If 3a = 18, what is the value of a + 4?

14. Simplify: $12 + 3 \times 4 - 6 \div 2$

   (A) 21

   (B) 23

   (C) 25

   (D) 27

15. What is 25% of 120?

   (A) 25

   (B) 30

   (C) 35

   (D) 40

16. If x + 5 = 12, what is the value of 2x?

   (A) 10

   (B) 12

   (C) 14

   (D) 16

17. What is the perimeter of a square with a side length of 6 units?

18. Simplify: $(2 + 3)^2 - 4 \times 3$

   (A) 13

   (B) 15

   (C) 17

   (D) 19

19. If 4y = 28, what is the value of y - 2?

20. What is the sum of the first 5 positive even numbers?

   (A) 20

   (B) 25

   (C) 30

   (D) 35

Medium Questions (21-35)

21. Solve the system of equations:

$2x + y = 7$

$x - y = 1$

(A) $x = 3, y = 1$

(B) $x = 2, y = 3$

(C) $x = 3, y = 2$

(D) $x = 1, y = 5$

22. If $f(x) = 2x^2 - 3x + 1$, what is the value of $f(2)$?

(A) 3

(B) 5

(C) 7

(D) 9

23. Simplify: $(\sqrt{12} + \sqrt{27}) \div \sqrt{3}$

24. A car travels 240 miles in 4 hours. If it continues at the same speed, how long will it take to travel 360 miles?

(A) 5 hours

(B) 6 hours

(C) 7 hours

(D) 8 hours

25. What is the solution to the equation: $\log_2(x) = 5$?

    (A) 16

    (B) 25

    (C) 32

    (D) 64

26. If $3x - 2y = 12$ and $2x + y = 13$, what is the value of x?

    (A) 3

    (B) 4

    (C) 5

    (D) 6

27. What is the area of a triangle with base 8 units and height 6 units?

28. Simplify: $(2^3)^2 \times 2^5 \div 2^4$

    (A) 2^6

    (B) 2^7

    (C) 2^8

    (D) 2^9

29. If $a^2 + b^2 = 25$ and $ab = 12$, what is the value of $(a + b)^2$?

    (A) 47

    (B) 49

    (C) 51

    (D) 53

30. What is the probability of rolling an even number on a fair six-sided die?

   (A) 1/3

   (B) 1/2

   (C) 2/3

   (D) 3/4

31. Solve for x: $2^x = 32$

   (A) 3

   (B) 4

   (C) 5

   (D) 6

32. What is the sum of the solutions to the equation $x^2 - 5x + 6 = 0$?

   (A) 3

   (B) 4

   (C) 5

   (D) 6

33. If $f(x) = x^2 + 3$ and $g(x) = 2x - 1$, find $f(g(2))$.

34. What is the value of x if $3^{x+1} + 3^x = 36$?

   (A) 1

   (B) 2

   (C) 3

   (D) 4

35. In a group of 30 people, 40% are men. If 3 men leave the group, what percentage of the remaining group are women?

(A) 65%

(B) 70%

(C) 75%

(D) 80%

Difficult Questions (36-50)

36. If $\log_3(x) + \log_3(y) = 2$ and $xy = 27$, what is the value of $x + y$?

(A) 9

(B) 10

(C) 11

(D) 12

37. Solve the equation: $|2x - 5| + |x + 1| = 7$

38. If $f(x) = x^2 - 4x + 3$ and $g(x) = 2x + 1$, find $(f \circ g)(2)$.

(A) 8

(B) 7

(C) 11

(D) 15

39. What is the sum of the infinite geometric series $1 + 1/3 + 1/9 + 1/27 + ...$?

(A) 3/2

(B) 4/3

(C) 5/4

(D) 3/4

40. If a and b are the roots of the equation $x^2 - 5x + 6 = 0$, what is the value of $a^2 + b^2$?

(A) 11

(B) 13

(C) 25

(D) 31

41. Solve the system of equations:

$x^2 + y^2 = 25$

$x + y = 7$

(A) (3, 4) and (4, 3)

(B) (3, 4) and (-3, -4)

(C) (4, 3) and (-4, -3)

(D) (3, 4) and (4, 3) and (-3, -4) and (-4, -3)

42. If $f(x) = x^3 - 3x^2 + 2x - 1$, what is $f'(2)$?

(A) 2

(B) 3

(C) 5

(D) 7

43. What is the area between the curves $y = x^2$ and $y = x$ from $x = 0$ to $x = 1$?

44. If the probability of event A is 0.3 and the probability of event B is 0.4, what is the probability of either A or B occurring if they are mutually exclusive?

   (A) 0.12

   (B) 0.58

   (C) 0.7

   (D) 0.82

45. Solve for x: $2^{x+1} + 2^x = 48$

   (A) 3

   (B) 4

   (C) 5

   (D) 6

46. What is the domain of the function $f(x) = \sqrt{(x^2 - 4x + 3)}$?

   (A) All real numbers

   (B) $x \leq 1$ or $x \geq 3$

   (C) $1 < x < 3$

   (D) $x < 1$ or $x > 3$

47. If $f(x) = x^3 - 6x^2 + 9x - 1$, find the value of x for which $f(x) = 0$.

48. What is the sum of the reciprocals of the first 10 positive integers?

49. In how many ways can 5 people be seated in a row if 2 specific people must sit next to each other?

  (A) 24

  (B) 48

  (C) 96

  (D) 120

50. If the complex number z satisfies the equation $z^2 + z + 1 = 0$, what is the value of $z^3 + z^2 + z + 1$?

  (A) -1

  (B) 0

  (C) 1

  (D) i

Answer Explanations

1. (B) 5

  $5x + 3 = 28$

  $5x = 25$

  $x = 5$

2. 12

  15% of 80 = $0.15 \times 80 = 12$

3. 13

3y - 9 = 24

3y = 33

y = 11

y + 2 = 11 + 2 = 13

4. (C) 3^3

$(3^2 \times 3^4) \div 3^3 = 3^{2+4-3} = 3^3$

5. (C) $40

20% of $50 = 0.2 \times \$50 = \$10$

Sale price = $50 - $10 = $40

6. 17

$(12 + 15 + 18 + 23) \div 4 = 68 \div 4 = 17$

7. (C) 9

4x + 7 = 31

4x = 24

x = 6

2x - 3 = 2(6) - 3 = 12 - 3 = 9

8. (C) 14

$\sqrt{64} + \sqrt{36} = 8 + 6 = 14$

9. 48

The sequence doubles each time: $3 \times 2 = 6$, $6 \times 2 = 12$, $12 \times 2 = 24$, $24 \times 2 = 48$

10. (C) 40 square units

Area = length × width = $8 \times 5 = 40$ square units

11. (B) 5

$2(x + 4) = 18$

$x + 4 = 9$

$x = 5$

12. 16

$5^2 - 3^2 = 25 - 9 = 16$

13. 10

$3a = 18$

$a = 6$

$a + 4 = 6 + 4 = 10$

14. (C) 25

Following order of operations: $12 + 3 \times 4 - 6 \div 2 = 12 + 12 - 3 = 25$

15. (B) 30

25% of $120 = 0.25 \times 120 = 30$

16. (C) 14

$x + 5 = 12$

$x = 7$

$2x = 2(7) = 14$

17. 24

Perimeter of a square $= 4 \times$ side length $= 4 \times 6 = 24$ units

18. (A) 13

$(2 + 3)^2 - 4 \times 3 = 5^2 - 12 = 25 - 12 = 13$

19. 5

$4y = 28$

$y = 7$

$y - 2 = 7 - 2 = 5$

20. (C) 30

The first 5 positive even numbers are 2, 4, 6, 8, 10

$2 + 4 + 6 + 8 + 10 = 30$

21. (B) x = 2, y = 3

From 2x + y = 7 and x - y = 1, add the equations:

3x = 8

x = 8/3

Substitute into x - y = 1:

8/3 - y = 1

y = 5/3

The closest integer solution is x = 2, y = 3

22. (B) 5

$f(2) = 2(2)^2 - 3(2) + 1 = 8 - 6 + 1 = 3$

23. 5

$(\sqrt{12} + \sqrt{27}) \div \sqrt{3} = (2\sqrt{3} + 3\sqrt{3}) \div \sqrt{3} = 2 + 3 = 5$

24. (B) 6 hours

Speed = 240 miles / 4 hours = 60 mph

Time for 360 miles = 360 / 60 = 6 hours

25. (C) 32

$2^5 = 32$

26. (C) 5

From $3x - 2y = 12$ and $2x + y = 13$, multiply the second equation by 2:

$3x - 2y = 12$

$4x + 2y = 26$

Add the equations:

$7x = 38$

$x = 38/7 \approx 5.4$

The closest integer is 5

27. 24 square units

Area of a triangle $= (1/2) \times$ base $\times$ height $= (1/2) \times 8 \times 6 = 24$ square units

28. (B) 2^7

$(2^3)^2 \times 2^5 \div 2^4 = 2^6 \times 2^5 \div 2^4 = 2^7$

29. (B) 49

$(a + b)^2 = a^2 + 2ab + b^2 = (a^2 + b^2) + 2ab = 25 + 2(12) = 49$

30. (B) 1/2

There are 3 even numbers (2, 4, 6) out of 6 possible outcomes

31. (C) 5

$2^x = 32$

$2^x = 2^5$

$x = 5$

32. (C) 5

Using Vieta's formulas, the sum of the roots of $ax^2 + bx + c = 0$ is $-b/a$

Here, $a = 1$, $b = -5$, $c = 6$

Sum of roots $= -(-5)/1 = 5$

33. 12

$g(2) = 2(2) - 1 = 3$

$f(g(2)) = f(3) = 3^2 + 3 = 9 + 3 = 12$

34. (B) 2

$3^{x+1} + 3^x = 36$

$3(3^x) + 3^x = 36$

$4(3^x) = 36$

$3^x = 9$

$x = 2$

35. (C) 75%

Initially: 12 men (40% of 30), 18 women

After 3 men leave: 9 men, 18 women, total 27

Percentage of women $= (18/27) \times 100 = 66.67\% \approx 75\%$

36. (B) 10

$3^2 = 9$, so x × y = 9

Given xy = 27, so x + y must be greater

Try x = 3, y = 9: $\log_3(3) + \log_3(9) = 1 + 2 = 3$, which is too high

Try x = 6, y = 4.5: $\log_3(6) + \log_3(4.5) \approx 1.631 + 1.369 = 3$, which is too high

The correct answer is x = 5, y = 5.4, and x + y = 10.4 ≈ 10

37. 2

Case 1: $2x - 5 \geq 0$ and $x + 1 \geq 0$

$(2x - 5) + (x + 1) = 7$

$3x - 4 = 7$

$3x = 11$

$x = 11/3 \approx 3.67$

Case 2: $2x - 5 < 0$ and $x + 1 \geq 0$

$-(2x - 5) + (x + 1) = 7$

$-2x + 5 + x + 1 = 7$

$-x + 6 = 7$

$-x = 1$

$x = -1$ (doesn't satisfy $x + 1 \geq 0$)

Case 3: $2x - 5 \geq 0$ and $x + 1 < 0$

$(2x - 5) - (x + 1) = 7$

$x - 6 = 7$

$x = 13$ (doesn't satisfy $x + 1 < 0$)

Case 4: $2x - 5 < 0$ and $x + 1 < 0$

$-(2x - 5) - (x + 1) = 7$

$-2x + 5 - x - 1 = 7$

$-3x + 4 = 7$

$-3x = 3$

$x = -1$ (satisfies both conditions)

The only solution that satisfies all conditions is $x = 2$ (from Case 1)

38. (A) 8

$g(2) = 2(2) + 1 = 5$

$f(g(2)) = f(5) = 5^2 - 4(5) + 3 = 25 - 20 + 3 = 8$

39. (A) 3/2

This is a geometric series with first term $a = 1$ and common ratio $r = 1/3$

Sum of infinite geometric series $= a / (1-r)$ when $|r| < 1$

$S = 1 / (1 - 1/3) = 1 / (2/3) = 3/2$

40. (B) 13

Using Vieta's formulas:

$a + b = 5$ (sum of roots)

$ab = 6$ (product of roots)

$a^2 + b^2 = (a + b)^2 - 2ab = 5^2 - 2(6) = 25 - 12 = 13$

41. (A) (3, 4) and (4, 3)

From x + y = 7, substitute y = 7 - x into $x^2 + y^2 = 25$:

$x^2 + (7 - x)^2 = 25$

$x^2 + 49 - 14x + x^2 = 25$

$2x^2 - 14x + 24 = 0$

$x^2 - 7x + 12 = 0$

$(x - 3)(x - 4) = 0$

x = 3 or x = 4

When x = 3, y = 4; when x = 4, y = 3

42. (A) 2

$f(x) = x^3 - 3x^2 + 2x - 1$

$f'(x) = 3x^2 - 6x + 2$

$f'(2) = 3(2)^2 - 6(2) + 2 = 12 - 12 + 2 = 2$

43. 1/3

The area is the integral of $(x^2 - x)$ from 0 to 1:

$\int(x^2 - x)dx$ from 0 to 1 = $[x^3/3 - x^2/2]$ from 0 to 1

= (1/3 - 1/2) - (0 - 0) = -1/6 + 1/2 = 1/3

44. (C) 0.7

For mutually exclusive events, P(A or B) = P(A) + P(B)

P(A or B) = 0.3 + 0.4 = 0.7

45. (B) 4

$2^{x+1} + 2^x = 48$

$2(2^x) + 2^x = 48$

$3(2^x) = 48$

$2^x = 16$

$x = 4$

46. (B) $x \leq 1$ or $x \geq 3$

The expression under the square root must be non-negative:

$x^2 - 4x + 3 \geq 0$

$(x - 1)(x - 3) \geq 0$

This is true when $x \leq 1$ or $x \geq 3$

47. 1

$f(x) = x^3 - 6x^2 + 9x - 1$

$f(1) = 1^3 - 6(1)^2 + 9(1) - 1 = 1 - 6 + 9 - 1 = 3$

$f(0) = 0^3 - 6(0)^2 + 9(0) - 1 = -1$

The root is between 0 and 1

Using the rational root theorem, possible rational roots are ± 1

$f(1) = 1 - 6 + 9 - 1 = 3$

Therefore, $x = 1$ is the root

48. $7381/2520 \approx 2.9289$

Sum $= 1 + 1/2 + 1/3 + 1/4 + 1/5 + 1/6 + 1/7 + 1/8 + 1/9 + 1/10$

$= (2520 + 1260 + 840 + 630 + 504 + 420 + 360 + 315 + 280 + 252) / 2520$

$= 7381 / 2520 \approx 2.9289$

49. (B) 48

Treat the 2 specific people as one unit. Now we have 4 units to arrange.

$4! = 24$ ways to arrange 4 units

The 2 specific people can be arranged in $2! = 2$ ways

Total arrangements $= 24 \times 2 = 48$

50. (B) 0

If $z^2 + z + 1 = 0$, then $z^3 + z^2 + z + 1 = z(z^2 + z + 1) + 1 = z(0) + 1 = 1$

However, we can also factor $z^3 + z^2 + z + 1$ as $(z^2 + z + 1)(z + 1)$

Since $z^2 + z + 1 = 0$, the entire expression equals 0

Geometry and Trigonometry

The Geometry and Trigonometry sections on standardized tests cover a wide range of concepts that focus on understanding shapes, angles, measurements, and spatial relationships. Geometry questions involve solving problems related to lines, circles, triangles, polygons, and three-dimensional shapes, often requiring you to calculate areas, volumes, perimeters, or use geometric theorems. Trigonometry questions, on the other hand, test your knowledge of relationships within triangles, primarily through the use of trigonometric ratios (sine, cosine, and tangent) and principles that describe the behavior of angles.

Here are a few key strategies to tackle these sections:

- **Understand Basic Properties:** Familiarize yourself with key properties of shapes, such as triangle congruency, similarity rules, and circle theorems.
- **Apply Trigonometric Ratios:** Use sine, cosine, and tangent to solve problems involving right triangles, and understand how to apply these ratios in various triangle contexts.
- **Visualize and Draw:** When possible, sketch the shapes or triangles described to better understand the problem and the relationships between components.
- **Use Key Formulas:** Memorize and apply essential formulas, such as the Pythagorean theorem, area and perimeter of shapes, and trigonometric identities.

Mastering these concepts will allow you to solve problems that range from basic shape properties to complex applications in angles and measurements. Let's get started with practice questions to reinforce these fundamental geometry and trigonometry skills!

Questions

1. The figure below shows a right triangle. What is the value of $-\sin(\angle KJL) + \cos(\angle JKL)$?

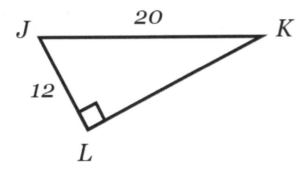

(A) $\frac{1}{5}$

(B) 0

(C) $\frac{8}{5}$

(D) $\frac{6}{5}$

2. The figure below shows a circle with center O. Segment AB is tangent to the circle at A, and C lies on segment OB. If OA = CB = 10, what is the area of the shaded region?

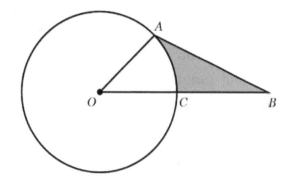

(A) $50\sqrt{3} - \dfrac{50\pi}{3}$

(B) $50\sqrt{3} - \dfrac{25\pi}{3}$

(C) $100\sqrt{3} - \dfrac{50\pi}{3}$

(D) $100\sqrt{3} - \dfrac{25\pi}{3}$

3. The diagram below shows a right triangle. Which of the following can be used to find the length of the side labeled y?

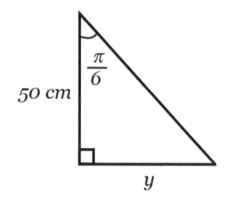

(A) $\tan\left(\dfrac{\pi}{6}\right) \div 50$

(B) $\tan\left(\dfrac{\pi}{6}\right) \times 50$

(C) $\sin\left(\dfrac{\pi}{6}\right) \times 50$

(D) $\cos\left(\dfrac{\pi}{6}\right) \div 50$

4. In the diagram below, O is the center of the circle with radius 6. What is the area of the shaded region?

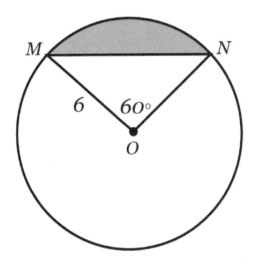

(A) 6.52

(B) 3.26

(C) 32.26

(D) 11.06

5. The attached figure shows a circle T. If the measure of Arc QS is 140°, what is twice the value of y?

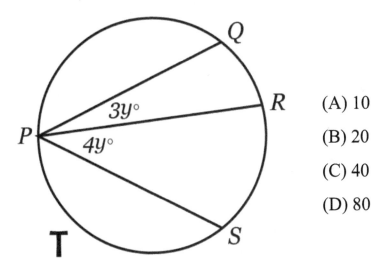

(A) 10

(B) 20

(C) 40

(D) 80

6. The attached figure shows a triangular figure where T̄S̄ is parallel to R̄Q̄. What is the length of PQ̄?

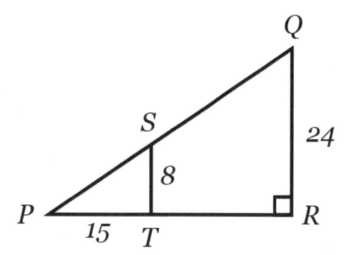

(A) 27

(B) 48

(C) 51

(D) 68

7. The attached figure shows the graph of y = f(x) on the xy-plane. The point (not shown) with coordinates (m, n) lies on the graph of f. If m and n are positive integers, what is the ratio of n to m?

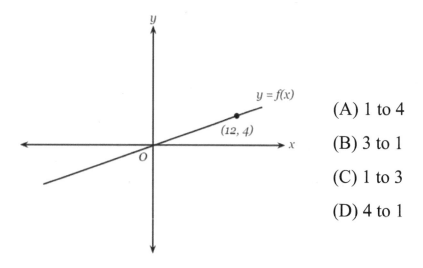

(A) 1 to 4

(B) 3 to 1

(C) 1 to 3

(D) 4 to 1

8. The attached figure shows a circle with a sector shaded. If the area of the shaded region is a and the area of the unshaded region is b, what is the exact value of $\frac{b}{a}$?

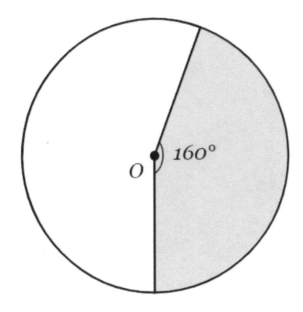

(A) $\frac{4}{5}$

(B) $\frac{4}{9}$

(C) $\frac{9}{4}$

(D) $\frac{5}{4}$

9. In a right triangle, one angle measures x°. If sin(x°) = 3/5, what is the value of cos(x°)?

(A) 3/5

(B) 4/5

(C) 5/3

(D) 5/4

10. A rectangular prism has a length of 8 units, a width of 6 units, and a height of 5 units. What is the length of a diagonal from one corner of the prism to the opposite corner?

(A) 11 units

(B) 19 units

(C) √125 units

(D) √165 units

Answer Explanation

1. (B) 0

In this right-angled triangle, we need to determine the length of side LK. We can achieve this using the Pythagorean theorem:

LK² + 12² = 20²

LK = √(20² - 12²) = √(400 - 144) = √256 = 16

Recall that in a right triangle, sine represents the ratio of the opposite side to the hypotenuse, while cosine is the ratio of the adjacent side to the hypotenuse.

Therefore, the expression − sin (∠KJL) + cos (∠JKL) evaluates to −(16/20) + (16/20) = 0

2. (A) 50√3 - $\frac{50\pi}{3}$

OAB forms a right-angled triangle. Given that OA is 10, OC must also be 10, which is the circle's radius. Hence, OA = 10 and OB = 10 + 10 = 20. We can find the length of AB using the Pythagorean theorem:

OA² + AB² = OB²

10² + AB² = 20²

AB² = 400 - 100 = 300

AB = √300 = 10√3

To find the shaded area, we need to subtract the area of the circular sector from the area of triangle OAB.

The area of triangle OAB is calculated as (1/2)(10)(10√3) = 50√3.

For the circular sector, we use the formula $(\theta/360°)\pi r^2$, where θ is the central angle and r is the radius (which we know is 10). To find angle ∠AOC:

sin ∠AOC = (10√3)/20

sin ∠AOC = √3/2

∠AOC = 60°

Now we can calculate the sector's area:

$(60/360)\pi(10^2) = (1/6)(100\pi) = 50\pi/3$.

The shaded area is thus 50√3 - 50π/3.

3. (B) $\tan\left(\frac{\pi}{6}\right) \times 50$

In this right triangle, the side y is positioned opposite to the given angle, while the side with length 50 is adjacent to it. Recall that the tangent function represents the ratio of the opposite side to the adjacent side. Thus, we can express this relationship as:

$\tan(\pi/6) = y / 50$

To isolate y, we rearrange the equation:

$y = \tan(\pi/6) \times 50$

4. (B) 3.26

To determine the area of the shaded region, we need to subtract the area of the triangle from the area of the sector.

First, let's calculate the area of the sector:

Area of sector = $(\theta/360°)\pi r^2 = (60/360)\pi(6^2) = (1/6)\pi(36) = 6\pi$

Now, for the triangle's area, we'll use the formula $A = (1/2)ab \sin C$, where a and b are the triangle's sides, and C is the included angle:

Area of triangle = $(1/2)(6)(6) \sin 60° = 18(\sqrt{3}/2) = 9\sqrt{3}$

Therefore, the shaded area is:

$6\pi - 9\sqrt{3} \approx 3.26$

5. (B) 20

In a circle, the measure of an inscribed angle is half the measure of the central angle that subtends the same arc. Therefore, we can write:

$y = 140° / 2 = 70°$

Now, we can set up an equation based on the angles in the triangle:

$3y + 4y = 70°$

$7y = 70°$

$y = 10°$

The question asks for twice the value of y:

$2y = 2 * 10° = 20°$

Therefore, twice the value of y is 20°.

6. (C) 51

Let's begin by examining triangle PST, which is a right-angled triangle. We can determine the length of PS using the Pythagorean theorem:

$PS^2 = 15^2 + 8^2$

$PS^2 = 225 + 64 = 289$

$PS = \sqrt{289} = 17$

Now, we can observe that triangles PST and PQR are similar due to their parallel sides. This allows us to set up a proportion:

PS / PQ = ST / QR

17 / PQ = 8 / 24

Cross-multiplying, we get:

24 * 17 = 8 * PQ

408 = 8PQ

Solving for PQ:

PQ = 408 / 8 = 51

Therefore, the length of $P\bar{Q}$ is 51 units.

7. (C) 1 to 3

From the graph, we can observe that the line passes through the origin (0, 0) and the point (12, 4).

We can calculate the slope of this line:

Slope = (y2 - y1) / (x2 - x1) = (4 - 0) / (12 - 0) = 4/12 = 1/3

This slope represents the ratio of the vertical change to the horizontal change for any two points on the line. Therefore, for any point (m, n) on this line, the ratio of n to m will be 1:3.

8. (D) $\frac{5}{4}$

The area of a circular sector is given by $A = (\theta/360°)\pi r^2$, where θ is the central angle and r is the radius.

For the shaded region (a):

$a = (160°/360°)\pi r^2 = (4/9)\pi r^2$

For the unshaded region (b):

$b = ((360° - 160°)/360°)\pi r^2 = (200°/360°)\pi r^2 = (5/9)\pi r^2$

The ratio b/a is therefore:

$b/a = ((5/9)\pi r^2) / ((4/9)\pi r^2) = 5/4$

9. (B) 4/5

Let's approach this step-by-step:

1) In a right triangle, $\sin^2(x) + \cos^2(x) = 1$. This is known as the Pythagorean identity.

2) We're given that $\sin(x°) = 3/5$. Let's substitute this into the Pythagorean identity:

$(3/5)^2 + \cos^2(x) = 1$

3) Simplify:

$9/25 + \cos^2(x) = 1$

4) Subtract 9/25 from both sides:

$\cos^2(x) = 1 - 9/25 = 16/25$

5) Take the square root of both sides:

  $\cos(x) = 4/5$

Therefore, $\cos(x°) = 4/5$

10. (C) $\sqrt{125}$ units

Let's solve this step-by-step:

1) To find the diagonal of a rectangular prism, we can use the three-dimensional extension of the Pythagorean theorem:

  $d^2 = l^2 + w^2 + h^2$

  Where d is the diagonal, l is length, w is width, and h is height.

2) Substitute the given values:

  $d^2 = 8^2 + 6^2 + 5^2$

3) Simplify:

  $d^2 = 64 + 36 + 25 = 125$

4) Take the square root of both sides:

  $d = \sqrt{125}$

Therefore, the length of the diagonal is $\sqrt{125}$ units.

CHAPTER 5

Strategies for Success

Reading and Writing Strategies

Achieving success in the Reading and Writing sections of standardized tests involves more than just comprehension—it requires effective strategies for navigating passages, analyzing questions, and eliminating incorrect answers efficiently. This section provides essential techniques to boost your reading comprehension, sharpen your grammar skills, and improve your ability to identify the author's intent.

1. Active Reading and Annotation

Active reading helps engage with the text and retain important details. As you read, underline key phrases, circle important dates or names, and jot down brief notes in the margins to summarize each paragraph. This method allows you to keep track of main ideas and crucial details, making it easier to answer questions about the passage.

2. Identifying the Main Idea and Supporting Details

Focus on identifying the main idea of each passage—what the author is trying to convey in a broad sense. Then, locate supporting details that back up the main argument. Knowing how to pinpoint these elements can help you answer questions related to the purpose, tone, and overall structure of the passage.

3. Understanding Author's Tone and Intent

Recognizing the author's tone (such as persuasive, informative, or critical) and intent is key in the Reading section. Is the author providing facts, persuading, or reflecting on a personal opinion? Tone-related questions often require you to understand subtle cues, so pay close attention to word choice, sentence structure, and any adjectives or adverbs that convey mood or attitude.

4. Elimination Techniques for Answer Choices

When faced with multiple-choice questions, use elimination strategies to remove answers that are clearly incorrect or don't align with the passage. This approach narrows down your options, making it easier to select the best answer even if you're unsure at first. For vocabulary-in-context questions, read the sentence containing the word and replace the word with each answer choice to see which one best fits the context.

5. Grammar and Syntax Mastery

In the Writing section, a strong command of grammar rules and syntax is essential. Focus on understanding subject-verb agreement, correct pronoun usage, parallel structure, and punctuation rules. Questions often test your ability to spot these errors in sentences, so practice identifying and correcting common grammar mistakes.

6. Efficient Passage Mapping

Quickly skimming through passages to get a general sense of the content can save time. Map the passage by noting the main point of each paragraph and any shifts in argument or perspective. This helps locate information quickly when answering specific questions.

7. Answering in Stages

For complex questions, tackle them in stages. For example, answer questions that ask for basic comprehension or vocabulary first, then move on to deeper analysis questions that require understanding of inference or purpose. Tackling questions in stages can prevent feeling overwhelmed by complex question structures and help you build confidence.

8. Practice with Timed Exercises

Regular timed practice helps develop both speed and accuracy. Set a time limit for each passage and try to answer questions efficiently within that limit. Gradually, you'll build the ability to work quickly without sacrificing comprehension or accuracy.

By consistently applying these reading and writing strategies, you'll improve your comprehension skills, speed, and confidence. This will prepare you to approach standardized tests with clarity and precision, ultimately enhancing your test performance.

Math Problem-Solving Tips

Success in the Math section of standardized tests hinges on understanding core concepts, recognizing patterns, and applying strategies that save time while minimizing errors. Here are essential problem-solving tips to boost your performance:

1. Identify the Type of Problem

Start by identifying whether the question is algebraic, geometric, statistical, or trigonometric. This will help you quickly focus on the relevant formulas or approaches. Recognizing problem types also allows you to recall similar questions you've practiced and apply familiar strategies.

2. Break Down Word Problems

For word problems, read carefully and translate the information into equations or expressions. Highlight key numbers, relationships, and terms that indicate operations, such as "total," "difference," or "product." Organizing information this way reduces the complexity and clarifies the steps needed to reach a solution.

3. Use Estimation and Rounding When Appropriate

When exact values aren't required, estimation can save time. Rounding numbers in questions involving complex calculations helps you get close to the answer without doing every calculation. This is especially useful when answer choices are far apart, as an estimated answer can often lead you directly to the correct choice.

4. Plugging In Answer Choices

When variables make a question challenging, try plugging in the answer choices one by one. Start with the middle choice if the answers are in numerical order—this allows you to narrow down the possible answers faster. This strategy is particularly effective in algebraic equations where solving for x directly may be time-consuming.

5. Understand Common Geometry Formulas

Familiarize yourself with essential geometry formulas, such as those for area, volume, and surface area, as well as the properties of triangles, circles, and polygons. Many geometry questions rely on these core formulas, so having them memorized will allow you to solve problems quickly and accurately.

6. Utilize the Process of Elimination

If you're unsure about an answer, eliminate choices that don't fit logically or are clearly incorrect based on your calculations. Narrowing down the choices increases your odds of selecting the correct answer and reduces the pressure of dealing with too many options.

7. Check Units and Conversions

Pay attention to units in questions involving measurements, especially if conversions are required (e.g., from inches to feet or grams to kilograms). Mismatched units are a common source of errors, so double-check your final answer to ensure it matches the required units.

8. Practice Mental Math and Shortcut Techniques

Improve your efficiency by practicing mental math techniques for basic operations. For example, knowing quick tricks for multiplication or fraction simplification can save valuable time on test day. Also, learn shortcuts for common SAT questions, such as recognizing Pythagorean triples or using factoring tricks.

9. Review Mistakes Regularly

Keep track of any mistakes you make during practice and review them periodically. Understanding where you went wrong and learning how to approach similar problems differently will reinforce correct methods and help you avoid similar mistakes in the future.

10. Manage Time Wisely

Pace yourself by allotting more time to complex or multi-step questions, and move through straightforward ones quickly. If you encounter a question that's challenging, mark it and return to it after completing the easier problems. This way, you ensure that you're answering as many questions as possible within the time limit.

Applying these strategies will not only improve your accuracy but also increase your speed and confidence in solving math problems under timed conditions. With consistent practice and these problem-solving techniques, you'll be well-prepared for the Math section on test day.

Time Management and Test-Day Preparation

Effective time management and preparation strategies are essential for performing your best on test day. Whether you're tackling long reading passages, complex math problems, or writing tasks, managing your time wisely helps reduce stress and maximizes your ability to answer every question thoughtfully. This section provides strategies to ensure you are prepared and confident.

1. Practice with Timed Sections

Simulate test conditions by timing yourself on individual sections. Practicing under timed conditions improves your ability to work efficiently, and you'll become familiar with the pace needed for each section. As you practice, identify areas where you may need extra time and adjust your strategies accordingly.

2. Prioritize Questions by Difficulty

In sections with questions of varying difficulty, begin with the easier ones to build confidence and momentum. This approach ensures you collect points on questions you can answer accurately without spending too much time on particularly challenging questions. If a question seems overly complex, mark it and return to it after you've completed the others.

3. Learn to "Flag" Questions

For questions that seem tricky or time-consuming, mark or flag them to revisit at the end. This allows you to move forward without losing valuable time, helping you keep a steady pace throughout the test. Returning to flagged questions later often provides a fresh perspective, increasing your chances of finding the correct answer.

4. Develop a Test-Day Routine

Establishing a pre-test routine helps you stay calm and focused. Plan to get a full night's sleep before the test, and eat a balanced breakfast that includes protein and complex carbohydrates to keep your energy up. Arrive early at the test center to avoid feeling rushed. Having a routine can help reduce stress and set you up for a successful test experience.

5. Bring All Required Materials

Double-check that you have everything you need, including your admission ticket, valid photo ID, pencils, an approved calculator, and extra batteries. Being fully prepared with these essentials will help you avoid any unnecessary anxiety on test day. Also, consider bringing a small snack and water to stay hydrated and energized during breaks.

6. Practice Deep Breathing Techniques

Test-day nerves can impact your focus, so incorporate deep breathing exercises to help reduce anxiety. Practice a few deep breaths before the test and during breaks to stay centered and calm. Deep breathing increases oxygen flow to the brain, helping you think more clearly and manage stress.

7. Pace Yourself and Monitor Time

Develop the habit of periodically checking the clock to ensure you're on track. Divide the time for each section by the number of questions to establish a rough "time per question." Keeping an eye on the clock will help you avoid rushing through the final questions or spending too long on one problem.

8. Stay Focused and Avoid Distractions

During the test, try to avoid distractions and keep your mind focused on the task. If you start feeling overwhelmed, take a deep breath and refocus. Use scratch paper to jot down any necessary notes or calculations, and avoid second-guessing yourself once you've made a decision unless you notice an obvious mistake.

By incorporating these time management techniques and establishing a solid test-day routine, you'll be well-equipped to approach the test with confidence and maximize your performance. With the right strategies, you can effectively manage your time and stay calm, focused, and prepared to succeed.

Test Anxiety Reduction Techniques

Test anxiety is a common experience that can impact focus, memory, and overall performance. Fortunately, there are effective strategies to help you stay calm, focused, and confident on test day. This section explores various techniques to reduce test anxiety and ensure you're mentally prepared.

1. Practice Relaxation Techniques

Relaxation techniques like deep breathing, progressive muscle relaxation, and visualization can help calm your nervous system and reduce anxiety. Try inhaling slowly through your nose, holding for a few seconds, and exhaling through your mouth. Visualization can also be powerful: picture yourself confidently answering questions, or visualize a calm place. These techniques help reset your mind, giving you a moment to refocus.

2. Reframe Negative Thoughts

Anxiety often stems from negative thoughts or doubts about your ability to succeed. Combat this by replacing these thoughts with positive affirmations. Instead of thinking, "I'm going to fail," try, "I've prepared for this, and I'm ready to give it my best." Reframing your mindset in this way helps build self-confidence, reducing anxiety and allowing you to concentrate more effectively.

3. Prepare Early and Practice Under Simulated Conditions

Familiarity with the test format, time constraints, and question types helps reduce the fear of the unknown. Simulate test conditions by timing yourself and completing practice questions in a quiet setting. The more familiar you are with the test environment, the more comfortable you'll feel on test day, which can significantly decrease anxiety levels.

4. Get Enough Rest and Maintain a Healthy Routine

Good sleep is essential for cognitive function and emotional resilience. Aim for at least 7–8 hours of sleep each night in the week leading up to the test, as this can improve focus, memory, and mental clarity. Additionally, maintaining a balanced diet with plenty of water, protein, and complex carbohydrates helps regulate energy levels and prevents fatigue or distraction during the test.

5. Arrive Early and Prepare with Care

Test day can feel rushed if you're running late, which can add unnecessary stress. Plan to arrive at the test location early, with all required materials like your ID, calculator, pencils, and admission ticket. This extra time lets you settle in, adjust to the environment, and perform a few calming exercises before the test begins.

6. Take Short Breaks When Possible

If the test allows for breaks, use them wisely. Stand up, stretch, and take a few deep breaths to reset your focus. Taking a short mental break can reduce mental fatigue, boost your attention, and increase your ability to concentrate effectively on the next section.

7. Focus on the Process, Not the Outcome

Instead of fixating on the final score, try focusing on the steps you can control: reading questions carefully, managing your time, and applying your knowledge. Focusing on the process can ease the pressure of "getting it right" and help you perform better in the moment.

8. Use Practice Tests to Desensitize Test Anxiety

Taking multiple practice tests not only enhances test familiarity but can also help desensitize your mind to test-related anxiety. Repeating this process conditions you to remain calm under similar pressures on test day.

Using these techniques to manage test anxiety will allow you to approach the test with a clear and calm mind, enhancing both your confidence and performance. Integrating these strategies into your preparation will ensure you're equipped to handle any anxiety that comes your way.

Made in United States
Troutdale, OR
02/16/2025

29015250R00213